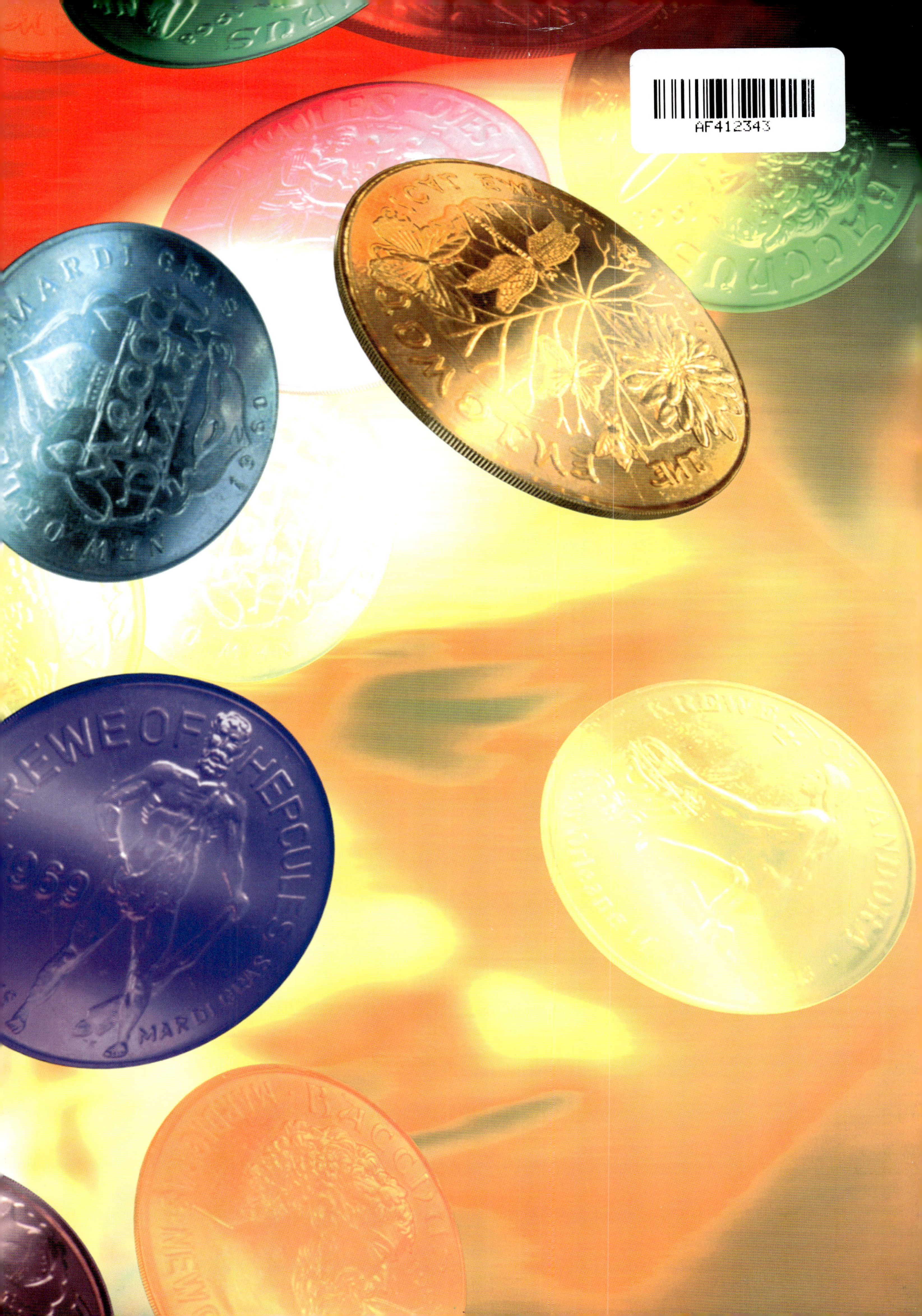

AF412343

The catalogue has been financed through the
Foundation Pinakothek der Moderne
Der Katalog wurde durch die
Stiftung Pinakothek der Moderne finanziert

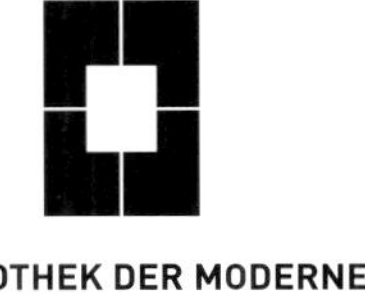

PINAKOTHEK DER MODERNE

MATTHEW WEINSTEIN

UNIVERSAL

PICTURES

KERBER

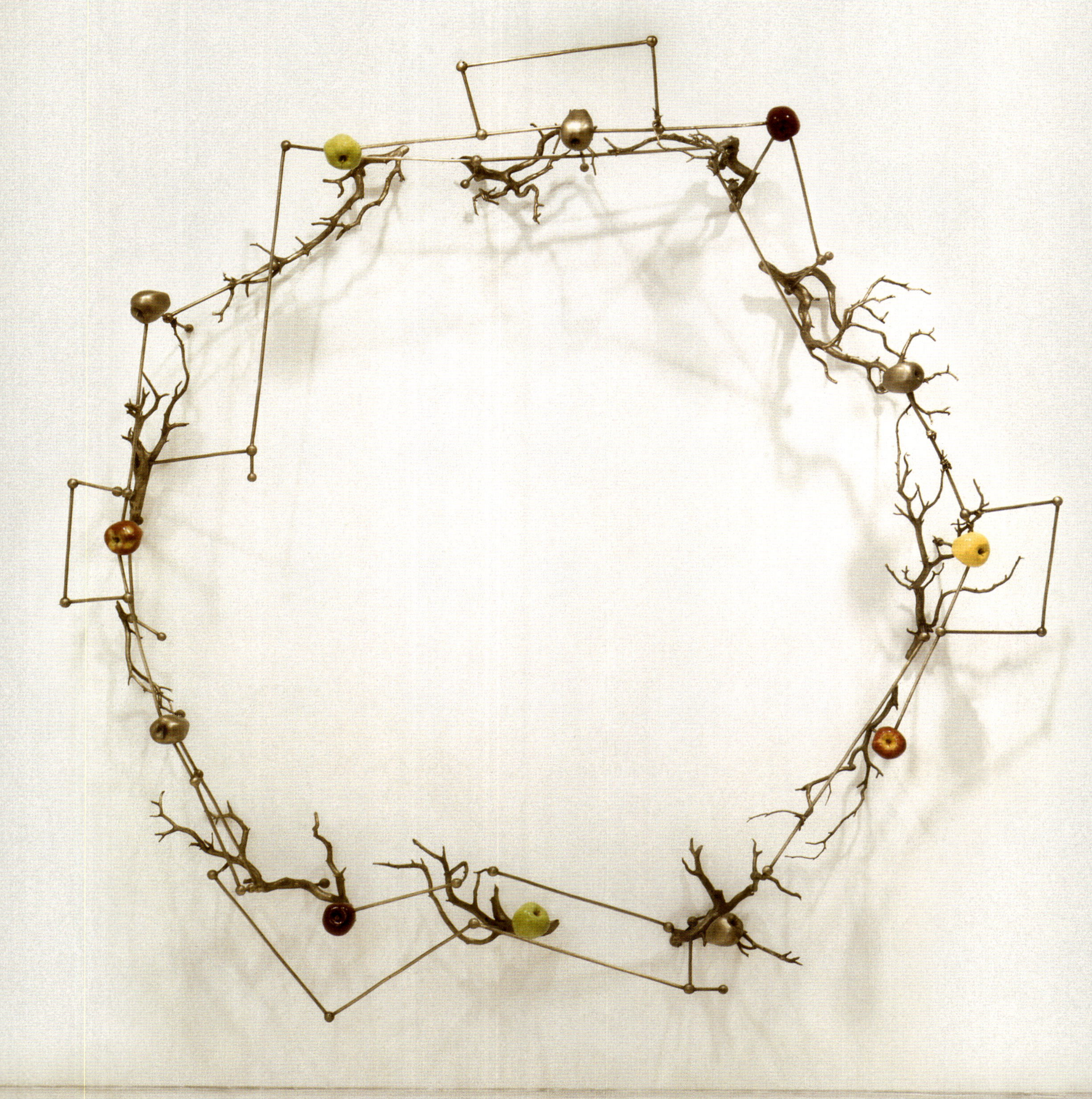

MATTHEW WEINSTEIN – UNIVERSAL PICTURES

In his first European solo museum exhibition, the American artist Matthew
Weinstein transforms spaces in the Pinakothek der Moderne into a
transcultural Garden of Eden. Colored Sand, sails and bronze frisbees take center
stage in this contemporary global dream. It is a leisure-wear paradise,
fashioned from a digital universe, which makes every metamorphosis possible:
from Adam's apple to the "Big Apple" all the way to golden Frisbees.
What counts is the rush of unleashed opportunity, the perfect body, eternal
youth, boundless communication and a deep-seated belief in high-tech,
which is as potent as exotic talismans and well-placed acupuncture needles.

The insignias of this American dream, including the coins that buy it, are sought
after more and more in every corner of the globe. In Weinstein's wonderland,
they pour into the lap of the viewer like a shower of golden rain; or a shower
of acid rain. The narrow border between the heavenly and the earthly,
the sacred and the profane and the imagined and the real is an ancient source
of evocation, which nourishes the theme-park of our iconic world.
This is a world in which the old is continually being transformed into the new,
in which the utopia of redemption is dreamed of and from which
a contemporary spirituality emerges that unites a potpourri of creeds and
elucidations and leaves all options wide open.

What explains the passion for surfaces? What is behind the craving for idols?
What is the difference between the desire for sacred idols and those created in the
dream factories of America's movie studios, which are constantly churning
out their idealized universal pictures?

Weinstein works within the border between the real and the imagined, the
universal and the vernacular, the dream and the nightmare. By so doing,
he unerringly evokes a critical and humorous encounter with the
theater of products and imagination, directly on the perimeter between pragmatic
facts and the need for individual reflection and reverie.

CORINNA THIEROLF

MATTHEW WEINSTEIN – UNIVERSAL PICTURES

In seiner ersten europäischen Einzelausstellung verwandelt der amerikanische
Künstler Matthew Weinstein Räume der Pinakothek der Moderne
in einen transkulturellen Garten Eden. Sand, Segel und Frisbees führen in die
Mitte eines Global Dream der Gegenwart. Das Paradies der
Freizeitkultur ist aus digitalen Welten generiert, die jede Metamorphose – vom
Apfel des Paradieses über den „Big Apple" bis zur golden glänzenden
Wurfscheibe – möglich machen. Was zählt, ist der Rausch
entfesselter Möglichkeiten: der perfekte Körper, die ewige Jugend, die
grenzenlose Kommunikation und ein Glaube, der auf High-tech ebenso vertraut
wie auf die Kraft der Talismane exotischer Länder und trefflich sitzende
Akupunktur-Nadeln.

Die Insignien dieses „American Dream" – darunter das Geld, für das man alles
erwerben kann – sind universell begehrt und scheinen dem Betrachter in
Weinsteins Wunderland wie ein mit Frisbees versetzter Goldregen in den Schoß
zu fallen. Wer mag sich da nicht an die Göttin Danae erinnern,
die als überaus fleischliche Verkörperung in den Bildern alter Meister die gülden
verklärte Befruchtung durch Zeus empfing? Die Grenze zwischen
Himmlischem und Irdischem, Heiligem und Profanem, Vorgestelltem und
Tatsächlichem ist von jeher die Quelle des phantastischen Stromes, aus dem die
Themen unserer Bildwelt entstehen. An dieser Quelle wird beständig
Altes in Neues verwandelt, an ihr wachsen die Utopien religiöser Erlösungen,
und aus ihr entsteigt auch die zeitgenössische „Spiritualität", die das
Potpourri der Religionen und Versuche von Aufklärung in sich verbindet und
alle Optionen offen lässt.

Wie erklärt sich die Lust an Oberflächen, was verbirgt sich dahinter? Was
unterscheidet die Jagd nach den Trophäen von Miami Beach und Big Apple oder
die Feier der idealisierten Bilder und Figuren amerikanischer Filmstudios
von der Sehnsucht nach den immer wieder hervorgeholten oder ausgetauschten
Götzen, die wie das Goldene Kalb umtanzt werden? Weinstein arbeitet mit
solchen zwischen Traum und Albtraum angesiedelten „Universal Pictures" und
evoziert genau an der Grenze zwischen objektiven Fakten und dem
Bedürfnis zu individueller Reflexion und Imagination eine kritische und
humorvolle Auseinandersetzung mit dem Theater der Waren und Imaginationen.

CORINNA THIEROLF

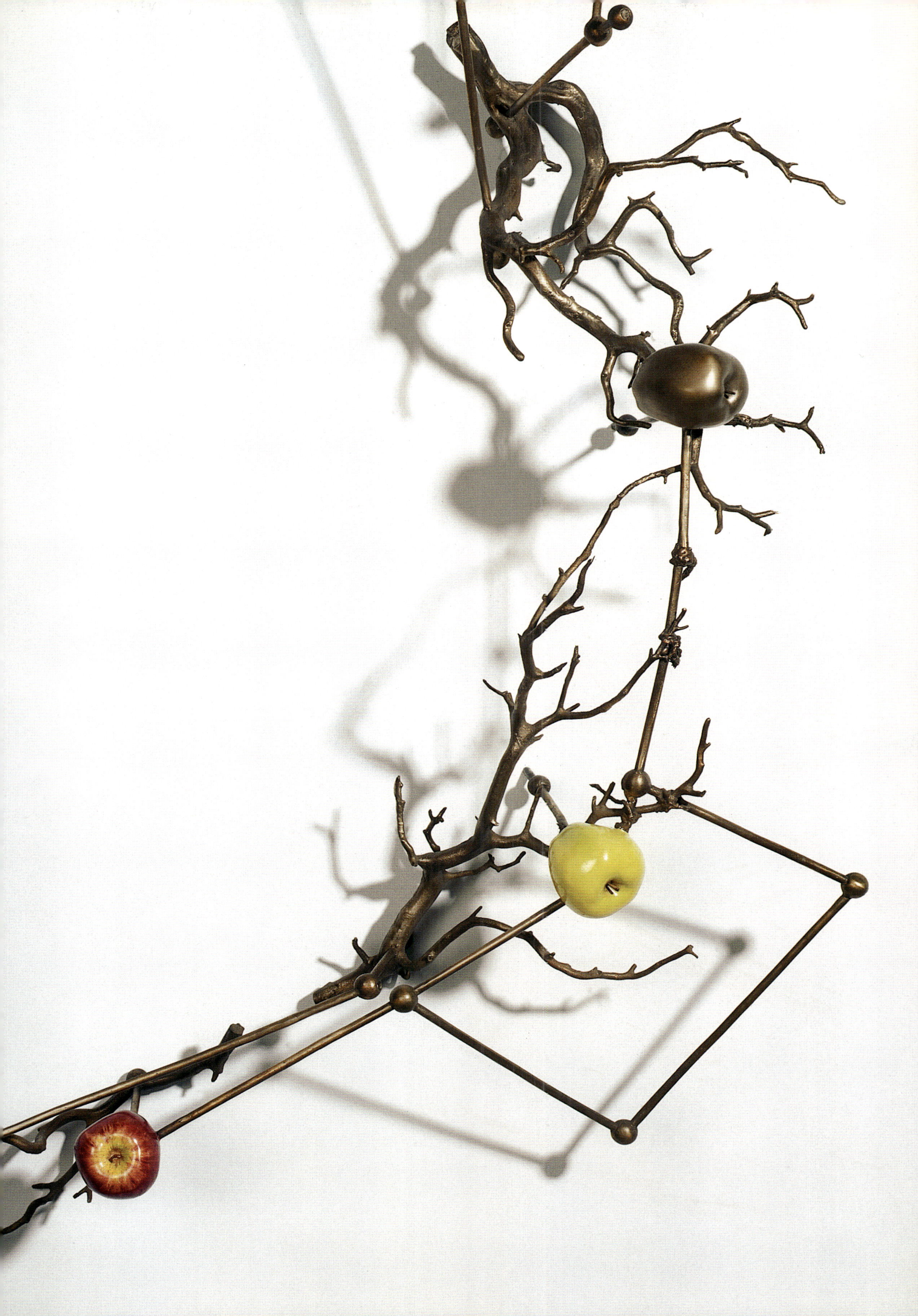

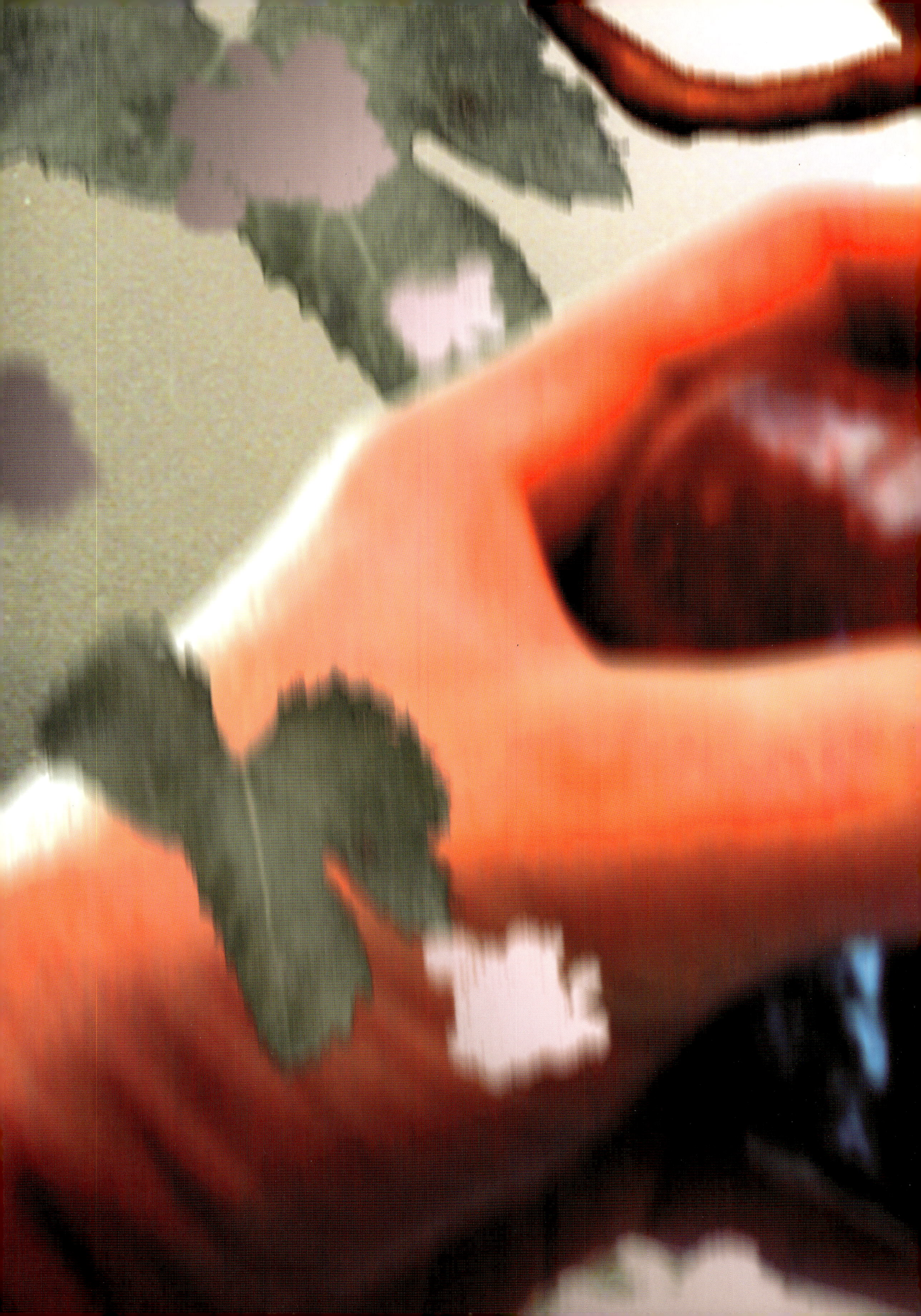

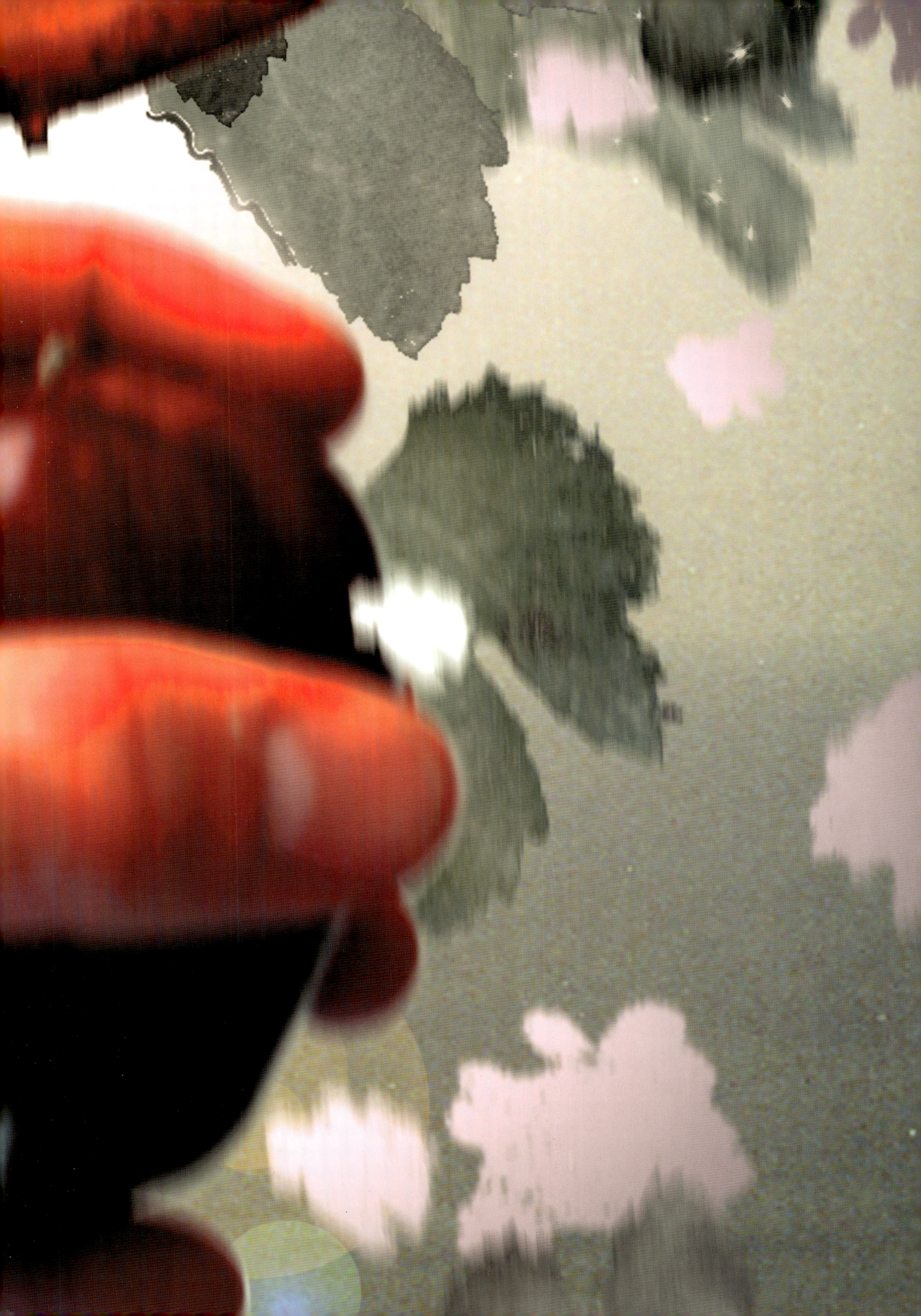

———————— the vision of perfection ————————

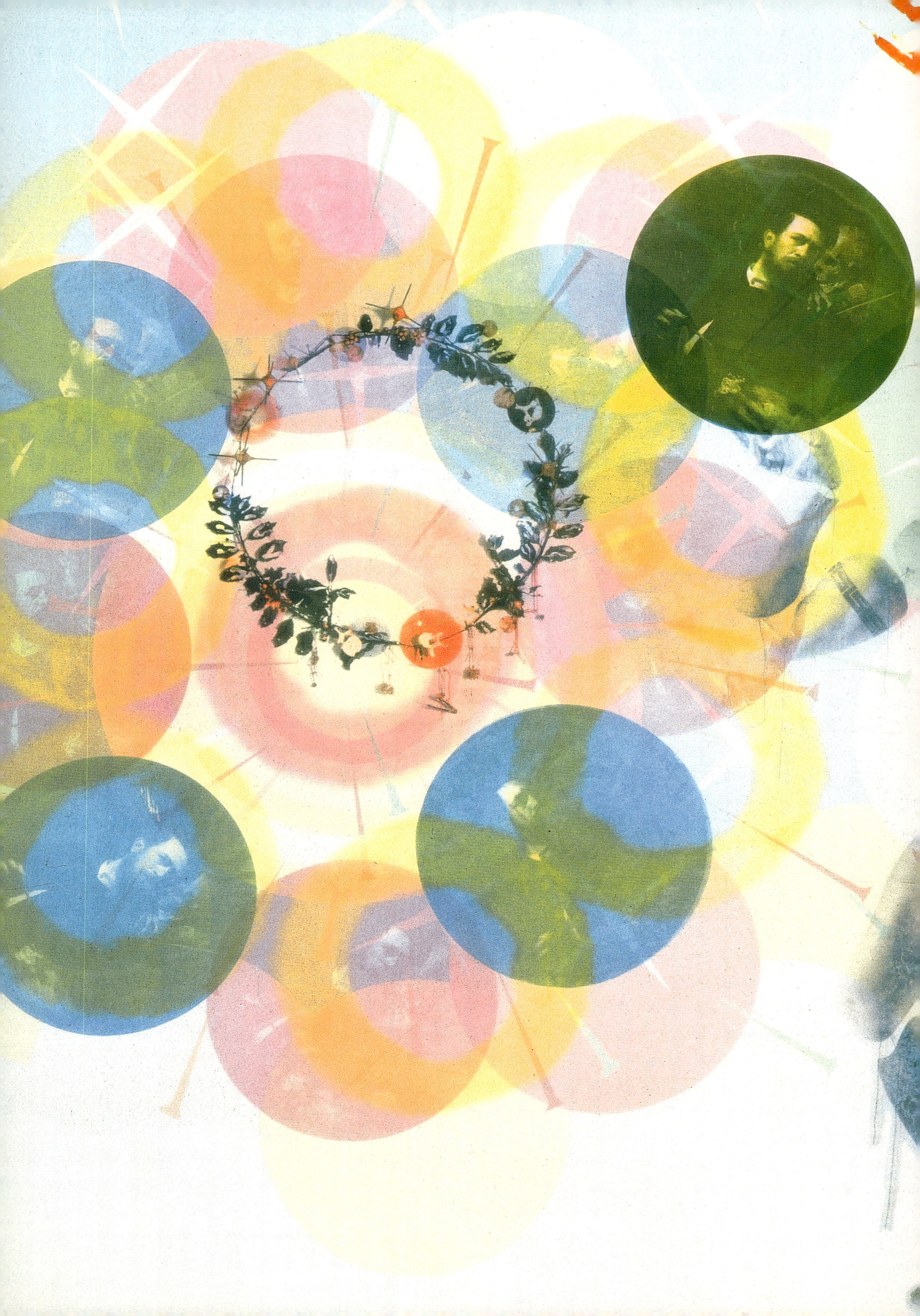

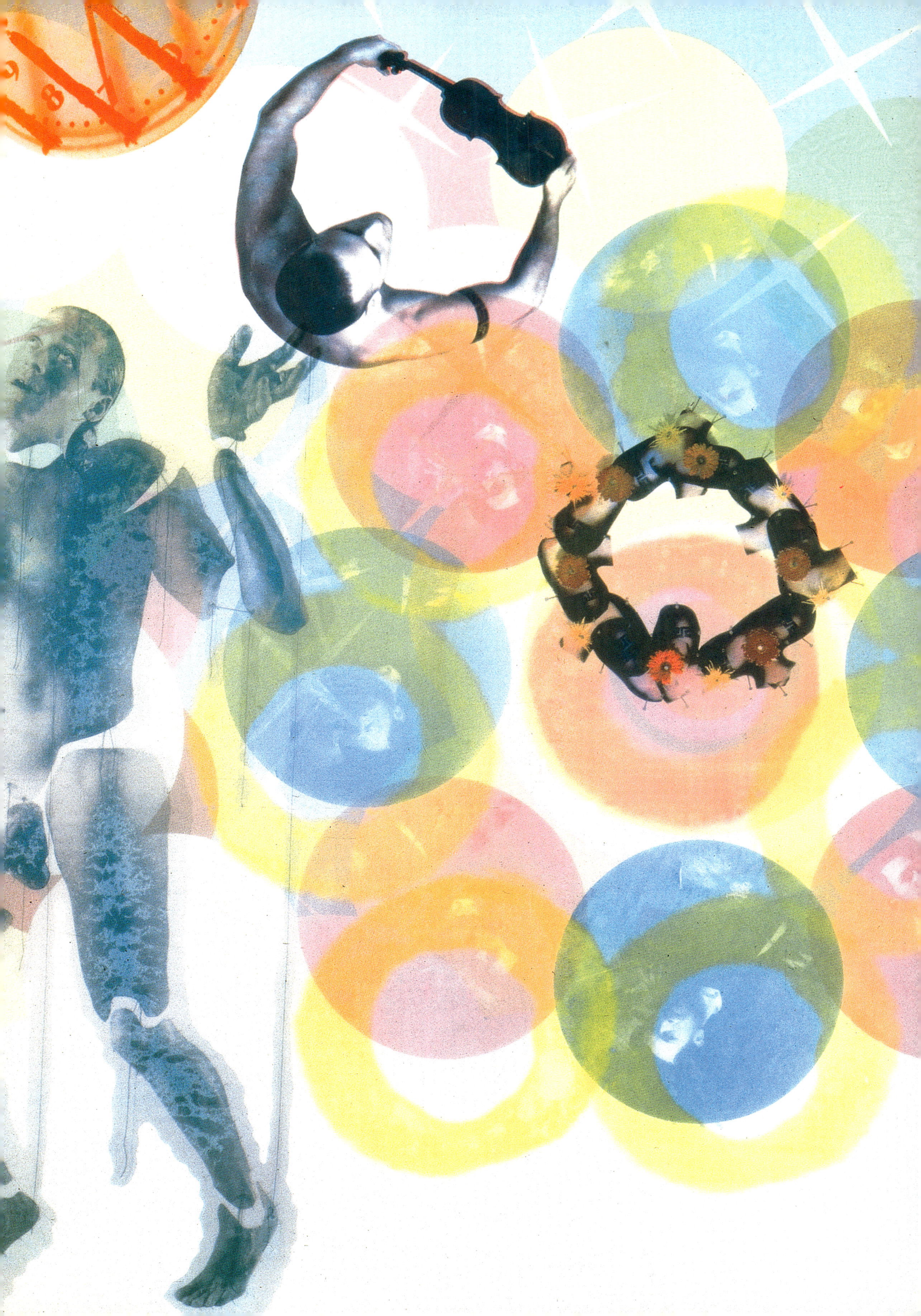

DER JONGLEUR
– EIN PROLOG

Viele Kunstwerke geben die mit ihrer Herstellung verbundenen Mühen nicht zu
erkennen. Daher bleiben etwa stereotype Gliederpuppen, die Malern den
rechten Weg zum perfekt dargestellten Körper weisen, oft im Verborgenen. Auch
ein Akrobat übt hinter dem Zirkuszelt, bis er seine Übung beherrscht. Der
Meister der Äquilibristik wäre eine Witzfigur, stünde er vor dem Publikum mit
leeren Händen, alle Bälle am Boden. Das Spiel ist ernst – und deswegen
weiß jeder Jongleur, dass er ein Spaßmacher ist, einer, der über die Schwerkraft
und den eigentlichen Lauf der Dinge seine Witze macht. Dem Jongleur
bleibt keine andere Wahl, als alle Bälle zu wählen, sie dem flüchtigen Leben für
Momente zu entreißen, um sie nach seiner Façon in Bewegung zu halten.
Eva, die sich für den verlockendsten, doch verbotenen Apfel entschied, prompt
aus dem Paradies vertrieben wurde und seither alle Hände voll zu tun hat,
mag ihm als biblische Stammmutter vor Augen stehen (S. 16/17).
Weinsteins Bild „Snowy Day" (S. 12/13) handelt von dem mühevollen Versuch,
das Unmögliche zu erreichen. Es beschreibt die Sehnsucht nach sinnvoller
Erklärung der Welt, damit auch nach Bildern, die dauerhaften Bestand haben. Es
handelt von der Suche nach beständigem Glück, davon, wie wir danach
greifen, ihm hinterherlaufen, es einzufangen versuchen und uns
letztlich dabei preisgeben wie der Künstler in diesem Selbstbildnis. Daher zeigt er
sich hier als lächerlichen Hampelmann, nackt und von scheinbar grenzenloser
Beweglichkeit. Sein gewaltiges Ziel verliert er nur deswegen nicht aus
den Augen, weil er sich in ekstatisch übersteigerter Konzentration auf die Vision
einer Perfektion einlässt, die er mit seinem verdreht nach oben gerichteten
Blick zu fixieren scheint. Zu den Geräten des Jongleurs gehört eine Uhr, die wie
ein Heiligenschein über dem Kopf schwebt; ihre Zeit läuft unerbittlich
ab, während die darauf angebrachten Geburtstagskerzen zuversichtlich brennen.
In anderen Tondi ist wiederholt Arnold Böcklins melancholisches
Selbstbildnis vor dem Violine spielenden Tod eingeschrieben, oder aber die Kreise
sind von leuchtend lockender Farbigkeit und bleiben innen leer.
Alle Kreisformen, Innbilder der Vollkommenheit, sind mit Insignien der
Vergänglichkeit verbunden, eine Bedrohung, die der ambitionierte Akrobat nach
Kräften von sich fernhält.
Der Jongleur, 1997 entstanden, ist ein dichtes Beispiel für den von Weinstein
entwickelten Motivschatz. Doch während der Künstler hier seine
Bälle allein in der Luft hält, wirft er sie in der Ausstellung „Universal Pictures" auch
dem Betrachter zu. CT

THE JUGGLER
– A PROLOGUE

The conventional jointed artist's dummy, which helps painters render a perfectly proportioned figure, remains backstage in the final work, like a juggler practicing behind a circus tent. The juggler would be a laughingstock if he were to stand before his audience with empty hands and all the balls on the ground.

Whether one is juggling tennis balls, images or chainsaws, juggling is a serious game. By teasing gravity, the juggler taunts the order of the natural world. The juggler has no choice but to uphold his concentration on all the balls, to snatch them so to speak from fleeting life in order to keep them, in his fashion, constantly in motion. Eve, who herself opted for the most auspicious yet forbidden apple to be then promptly ejected from paradise and from that time on having her hands full, my be considered the juggler's biblical progenitrix (p. 16/17).

Weinstein's painting, "Snowy Day" (p. 12/13), is a self portrait of the artist as a juggler. It deals with the unattainable search for perfect and lasting happiness through the creation of perfect meaning in a world of randomly firing signs. Perfect meaning is, after all, happiness for any artist; self explanatory yet subtle, ripe on the vine but not yet picked. The artist portrays himself as a naked and absurd dummy. He is grasping for meaning but constantly dropping the ball. In "Snowy Day", the artist's face is set in an expression of extreme and comic absorption centered in a vision of perfection. His juggler's gear includes a giant clock that hovers over his head like a halo, ticking away relentlessly while birthday candles, which have been placed on each number, burn on assuredly.

Arnold Böcklin's melancholic self-portrait with death playing the violin is repeated in one tondo, while other bright and alluringly colored circles remain empty. All of the juggler's balls are circular forms, visual embodiments of perfection, and all are allied with the insignia of transitoriness; a threat that the determined acrobat keeps at a distance.

This Juggler, completed in 1997, is a dense example of Weinstein's self-wrought motif treasury. Yet while in this painting the artist keeps all of his balls in the air, in the exhibition "Universal Pictures" he throws them at the viewer. CT

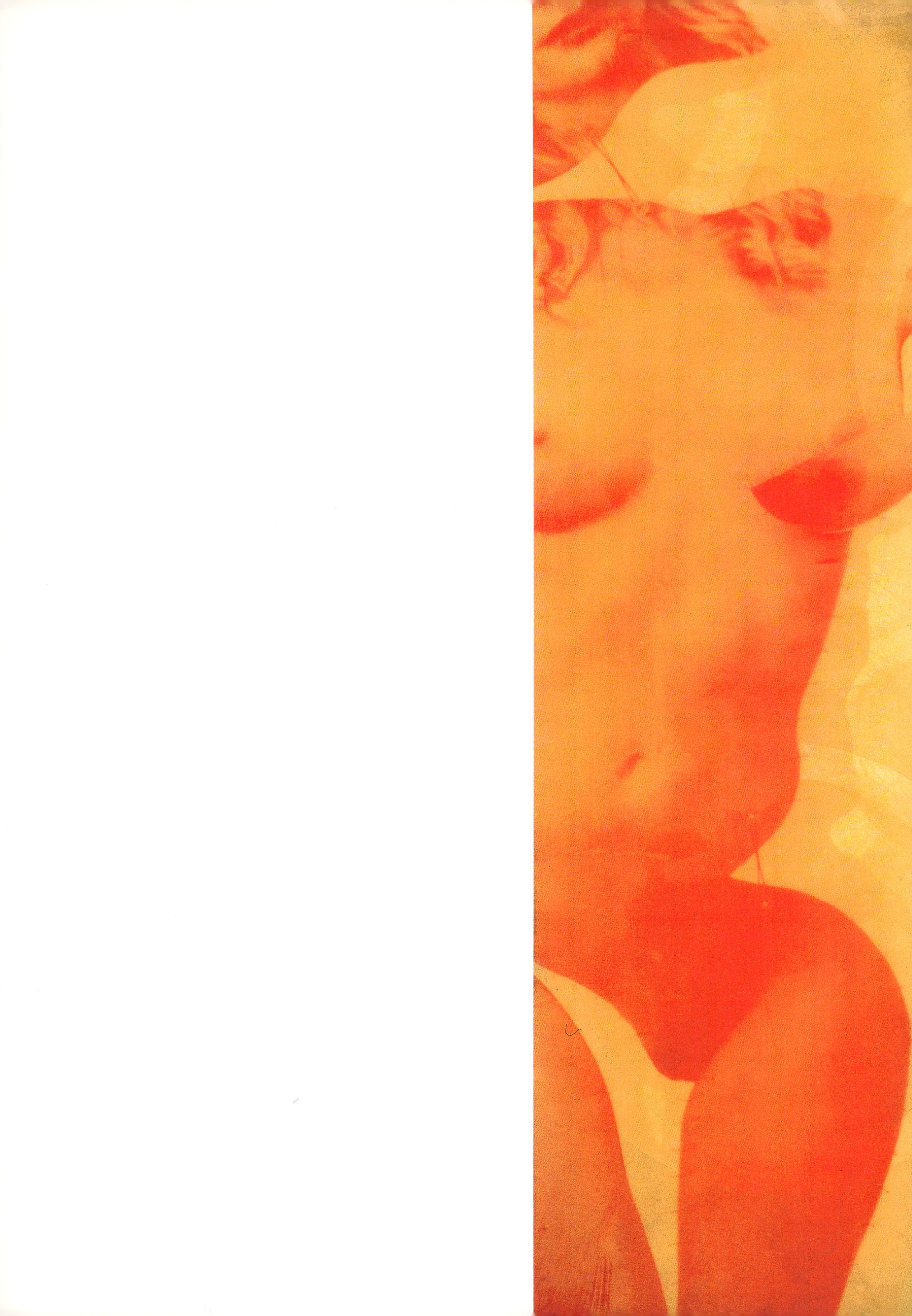

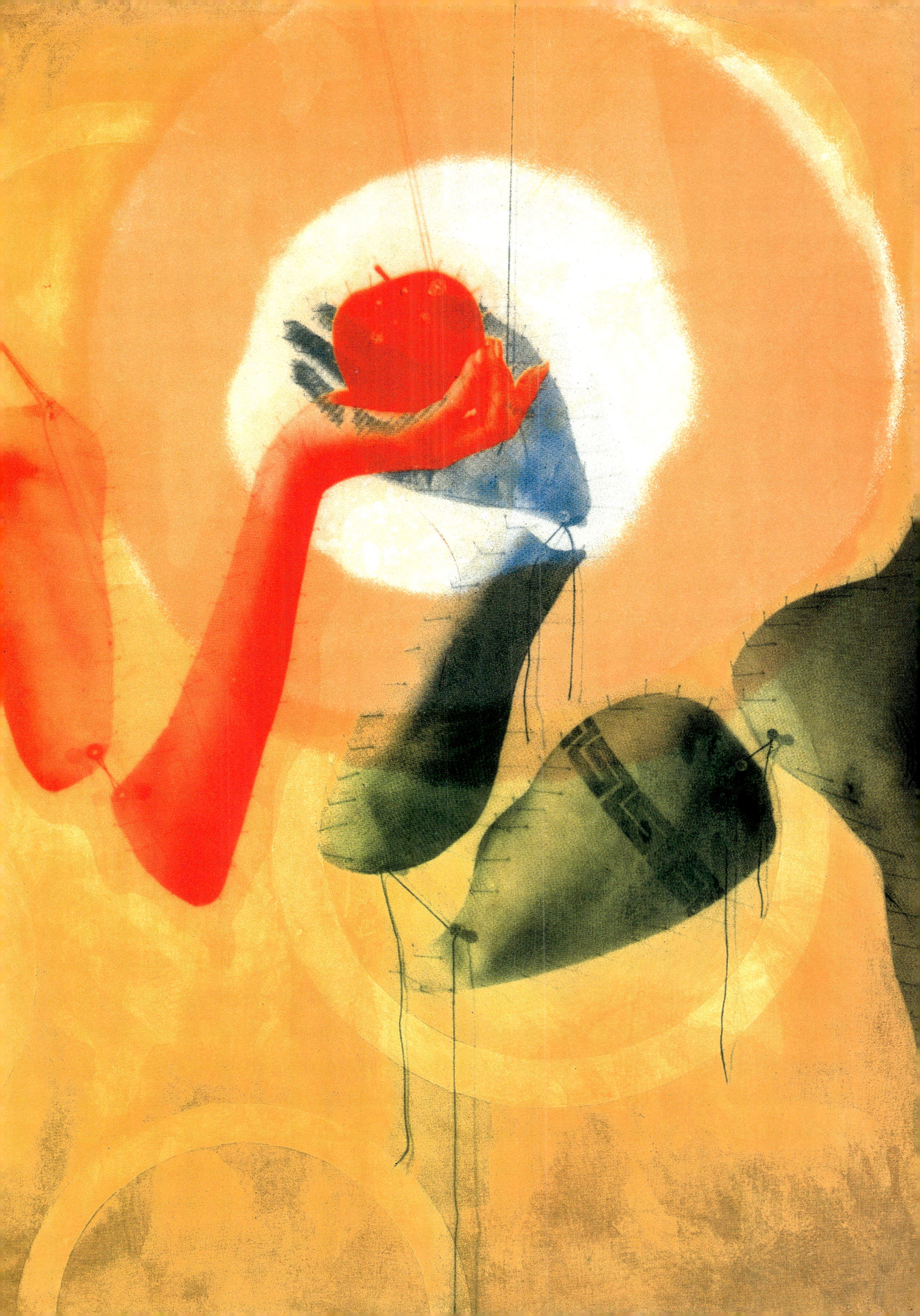

________ unidentified flying objects ________

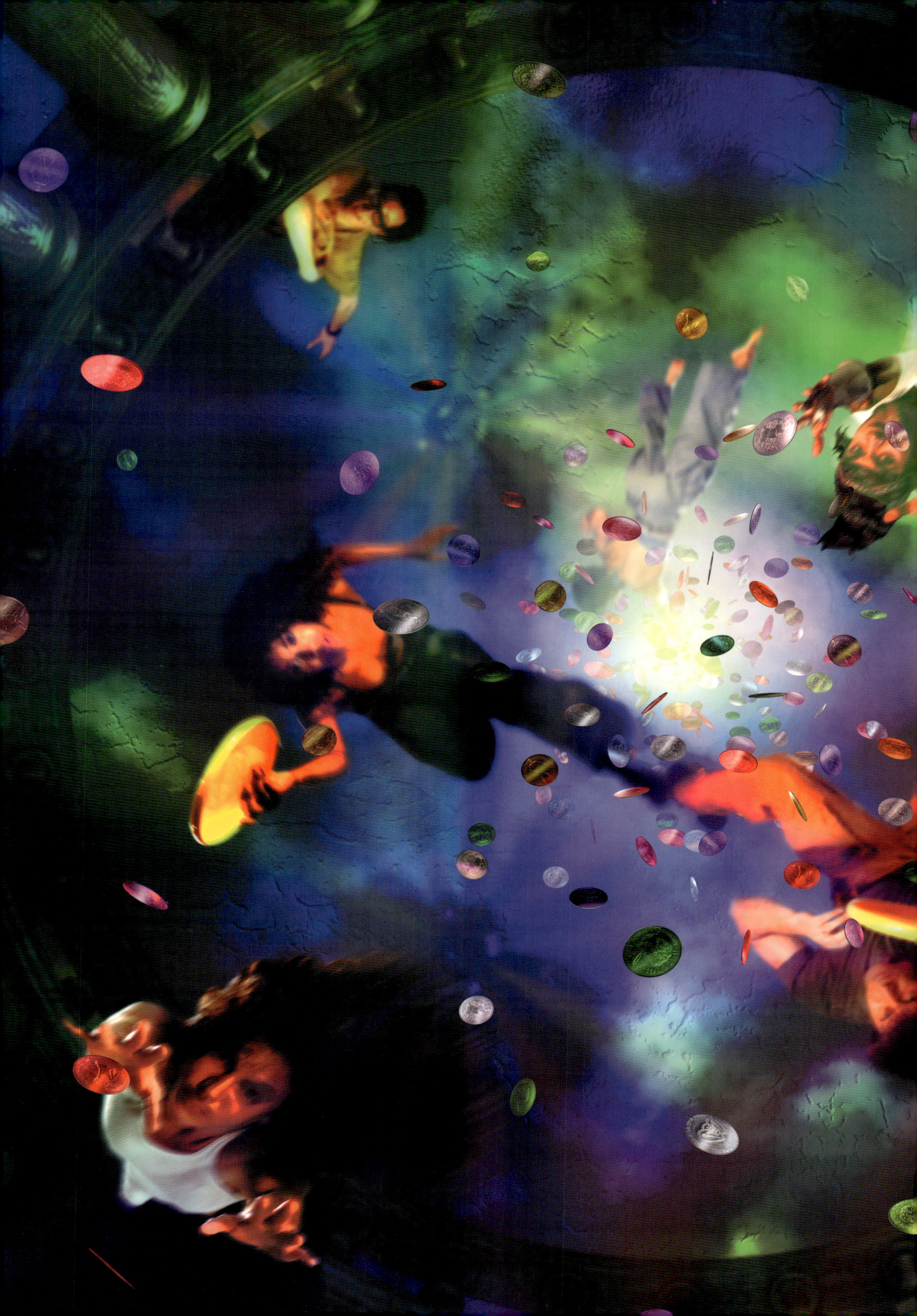

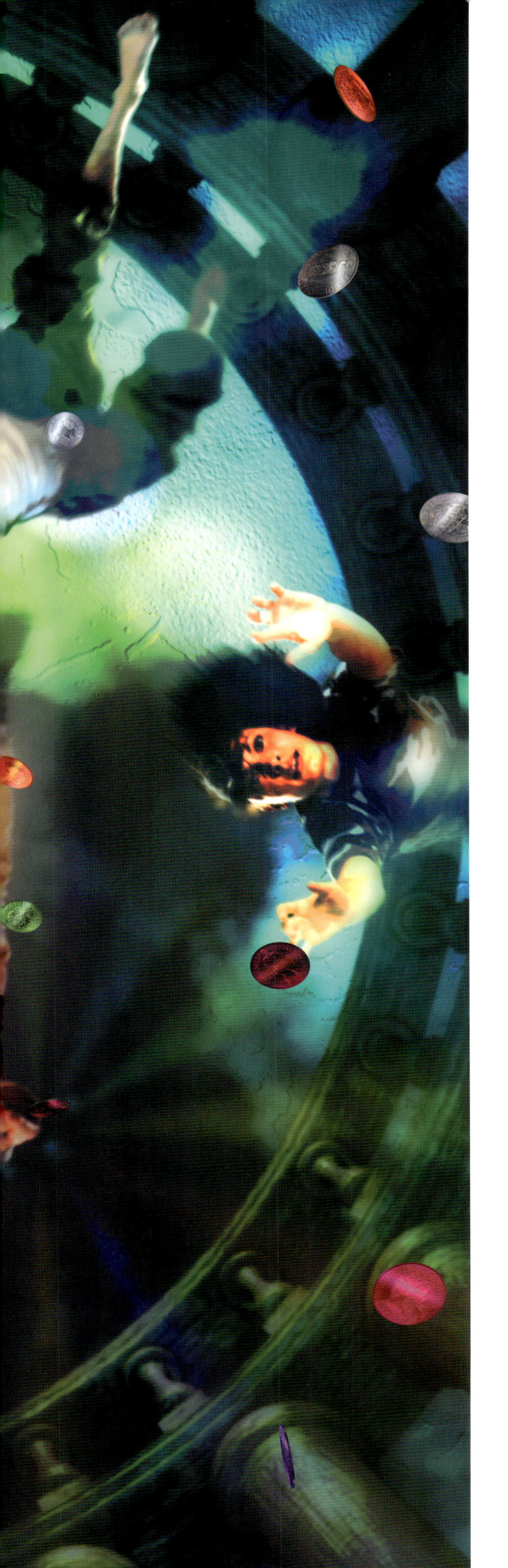

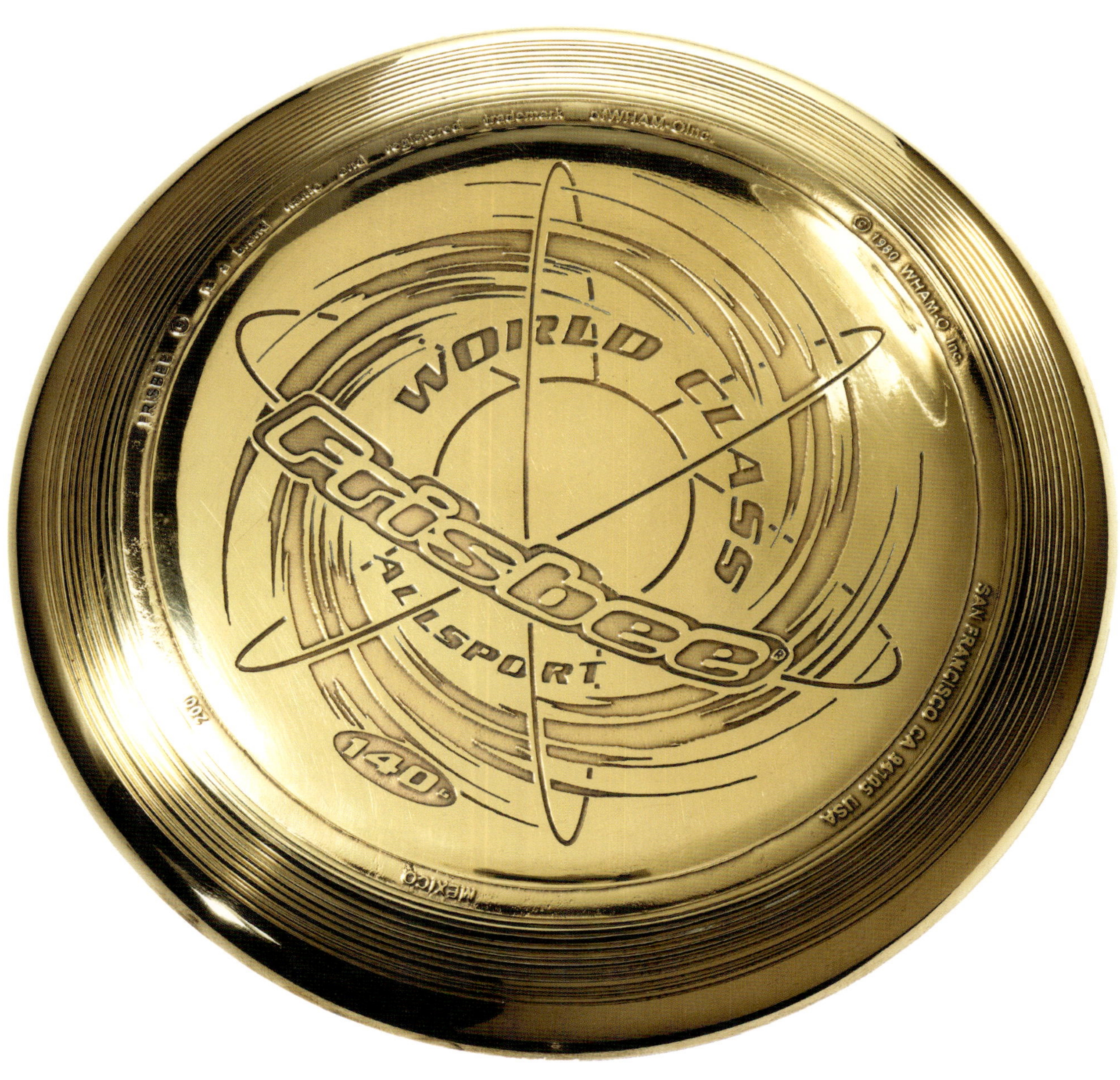

WORLD CLASS
frisbee®
ALLSPORT
140g
© 1980 WHAM-O Inc.
SAN FRANCISCO CA 94705 USA
MEXICO

FRISBEE – OR A LANDING
ON THE ROOF

"A hand catching a Frisbee – I love that image. A flying halo that laughs in the
face of gravity, an UFO with someone chasing it like crazy. The Frisbee is
such a potent symbol of America's longing to join the future while living in the
past, to hang on to the technological and cultural optimism of the 60's.
It's like a dream from another world, a little hallucination of physical perfection,
way up there, born of its own circular movement. The Frisbee has the power of a
fetish that sets bodies in motion. We simply have to catch it, we can't resist it."
For the artist, grasping the Frisbee brings with it "a moment of unjaded pleasure."
He describes the Frisbee as a kind of Proustian madelaine, dipped into
sand, salt water and the freshly cut green grass of summer. It transports our adult
bodies back into an earlier time of their own histories. Weinstein creates
enormous Frisbees on the ground out of poured unfixed sand whose fragility
makes physical contact lethal for the object and would negate days of painstaking
labor (p. 26/27). He also makes Frisbees out of glistening polished bronze
which, if hurled, would be lethal for the receiver (p. 22). However, both works
embrace a remarkable intersection between appearance and potential
disappearance, which can be interpreted as an aesthetic experiential translation of
catching and throwing.
The size of the bronze Frisbee in "Bell" corresponds to the exact size of the copied
original, whereas color, material, weight and technique are completely
different. "Bell", due to it's shine, takes on the aura of a halo that has fallen to
earth, which is emphasized by the work's title. The commonplace
aspect of the object takes backseat to a plainly manifest sacral component, as if
the original object was given a particular consecration in more divine regions.
The commercial product, at one time quite earthly, is now consequently marked
as if from a cosmic eddy.
The rejoinder to the sound material presence of the bronze Frisbee is the
monumental Frisbee in sand. The grains of sand lie loosely next to
each other and together form an image like pixels on a computer screen. The
integrity of the sand image is fragile, transitory (it is destroyed when it is
de-installed) and fleeting, like the flying Frisbee during a game. It has the form
of a mandala (Sanskrit: circle), those predominantly four-sided meditation
images developed within the tantric Buddhist tradition, which contain pictorial
or abstract depictions as part of a consecrated geometry.
Traditional sand mandalas are fashioned by Tibetan monks according to
strict rules. They are then blessed and destroyed, as an expression of the
impermanence of all living things. Even so, the sand remains within the larger

FRISBEE – ODER EINE LANDUNG AUF DEM DACH

„Eine Hand, die nach einem Frisbee greift – ich liebe dieses Bild. Da ist ein fliegendes Spielzeug, ein der Schwerkraft trotzender Heiligenschein, ein UFO – und eine Person, die diesem Ding wie verrückt hinterher jagt. Das Frisbee ist ein prägnantes Bild für das amerikanische Bedürfnis, die Zukunft zu erreichen, während wir doch in der Vergangenheit leben, den Idealen der sechziger Jahre nachhängen, jener vom Pop imprägnierten Zeit, in der es auch noch einen ungebrochenen Technik- und Wissenschaftsoptimismus gab, und aus der das Frisbee überlebt hat. Es ist wie ein Traum von einer anderen Welt, eine kleine Halluzination, es scheint, als sei es hoch oben aus seiner eigenen kreisförmigen Bewegung heraus geboren. Dem Frisbee wohnt die Kraft eines Fetischs inne, es setzt Körper in Bewegung. Wir müssen das Frisbee einfach bekommen, wir müssen es fangen, danach greifen."

Das Greifen nach dem Frisbee im Spiel bringt, so der Künstlers, einen „Moment entspannten Glücks", der vom fast schwerelosen Flug des Gegenstandes durch Raum und Zeit herrühren mag, an dem die Spieler teilhaben. Doch Weinsteins Frisbees (sie sind aus Sand „gemalt" oder aus glänzend polierter Bronze hergestellt) fliegen nicht und würden durch eine Berührung unweigerlich in ihrer Unversehrtheit beeinträchtigt. Beide Werke enthalten eine bemerkenswerte Verschränkung von Präsenz und potentiellem Verschwinden, was als ästhetische Übersetzung der Erfahrung vom Erhalten und Abgeben des Frisbees im Spiel gedeutet werden kann: Die Größe des Frisbees in „Bell" (S. 22) entspricht exakt dem abgeformten Original aus Plastik während sich das schwere und wertvolle Material sowie die sorgfältige Politur davon unterscheiden. Anstelle des Gebrauchsaspektes tritt im Bronzefrisbee eine auch vom Titel unterstützte sakrale Komponente in den Vordergrund, so, als habe der ursprüngliche Gegenstand in himmlischen Sphären eine besondere Weihe erhalten. Nun wirkt die Scheibe tatsächlich wie ein auf die Erde gefallener Heiligenschein. Das einst überaus irdische Markenzeichen liest sich folgerichtig wie die Aufprägung eines kosmischen Wirbels.

In der monumentalen Bodenarbeit (S. 26/27) liegen hingegen unzählige Sandkörnern nur lose auf- und nebeneinander. Im Gegensatz zur Bronzeskulptur ist die Integrität dieses Werks fragil, vergänglich, sie ist flüchtig, wie das Frisbee im Spiel. Es hat die Gestalt eines Mandala (Sanskrit: Kreis), jener im tantristischen Buddhismus entwickelten, meist viereckigen Meditationsbilder, deren bildhafte oder abstrakte Darstellungen in eine als heilig verehrte Geometrie eingebunden sind. Das traditionelle Mandala wird nach festen Regeln von Mönchen hergestellt, geweiht und wieder zerstört, um damit die Vergänglichkeit alles Lebendigen zu zeigen. Dennoch bleibt der Sand im vitalen Kreislauf,

energy-cycle as the swept-together mixture, which was once a concrete and
curative image, is strewn upon the river so that its formerly localized
potency can be made available to every being. In his sand Frisbee, Weinstein has
united a mass-produced mundane object with a sacred form – a generally
forbidden activity within the house rules of the sacred and the profane.
Weinstein's transgression could be interpreted as a sin by the faithful and as a
frustrating ambiguity for those seeking a path to the spirit. The transformation of
the Frisbee into an apparently holy object exposes sainthood as a human
fabrication; but before we can ascribe a cynical intent to Weinstein's work, we
must remember that it was painstakingly created only to offer up
experience and then be destroyed. In this way, like the Buddhist mandala, it exists
as an object which is empathic to the human condition.
Within this boundary-infringement, which carries with it a congruent
overlapping of two initially separate territories, there is an empirical possibility
that is comparable to a hallucination; the Frisbee of visionary spirits
that might appear as a radiance over the heads of sportsmen who,
with their conditioned bodies, experience the dream of an endless summer and
an endless adolescence for a few moments. The understanding of what
a Frisbee is, from a pragmatic standpoint, is surpassed in this state where sensorial
seeing and "inner seeing" overlap. Furthermore, the floor-based structure,
constructed from thousands of sand pixels, is about a virtual reality in
which identity is dissolved into dots of information which,
depending on their frequency, allow for a higher or lower level of reality.
The title of the piece, "Ed Headrick, Designer of the Modern Frisbee, Dies at 78",
defines the sand Frisbee as a tribute to the inventor of the "flying saucer",
who died on August 12, 2002. In 1957, Headrick was faced with
the task of finding a new use for a whole warehouse full of plastic that was
originally intended for the manufacture of hula-hoops (another circle),
which had gone out of style. Headrick landed a big hit with the Frisbee, a product
to which, as he related in an interview, he devoted body and soul.
Just about a year before he died he made an interesting association between the
Frisbee and the afterlife: "We used to say the Frisbee is really a religion
– 'Frisbyterians' we'd call ourselves. When we die, we don't go to purgatory.
We just land up on the roof and lay there."
A landing on the roof? A golden, fallen halo in a secular museum? A fragile
monument to the perpetuity of death? A flickering between appearing
and disappearing? "We can only," according to Weinstein, "approach the frontiers
of life through hallucinations." Incredibly precise images emerge
within the vision. CT

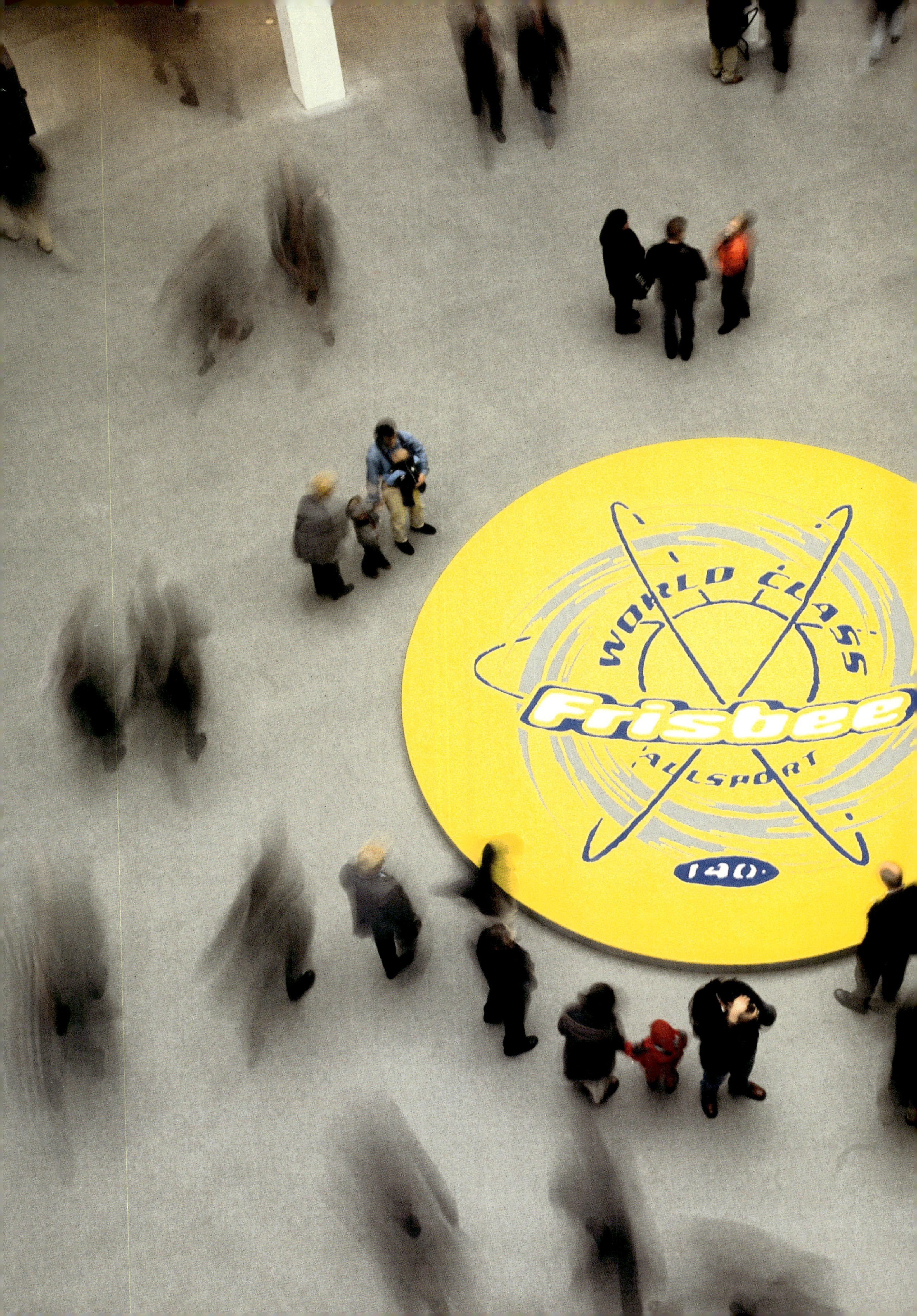

WORLD CLASS
Frisbee
ALLSPORT
140

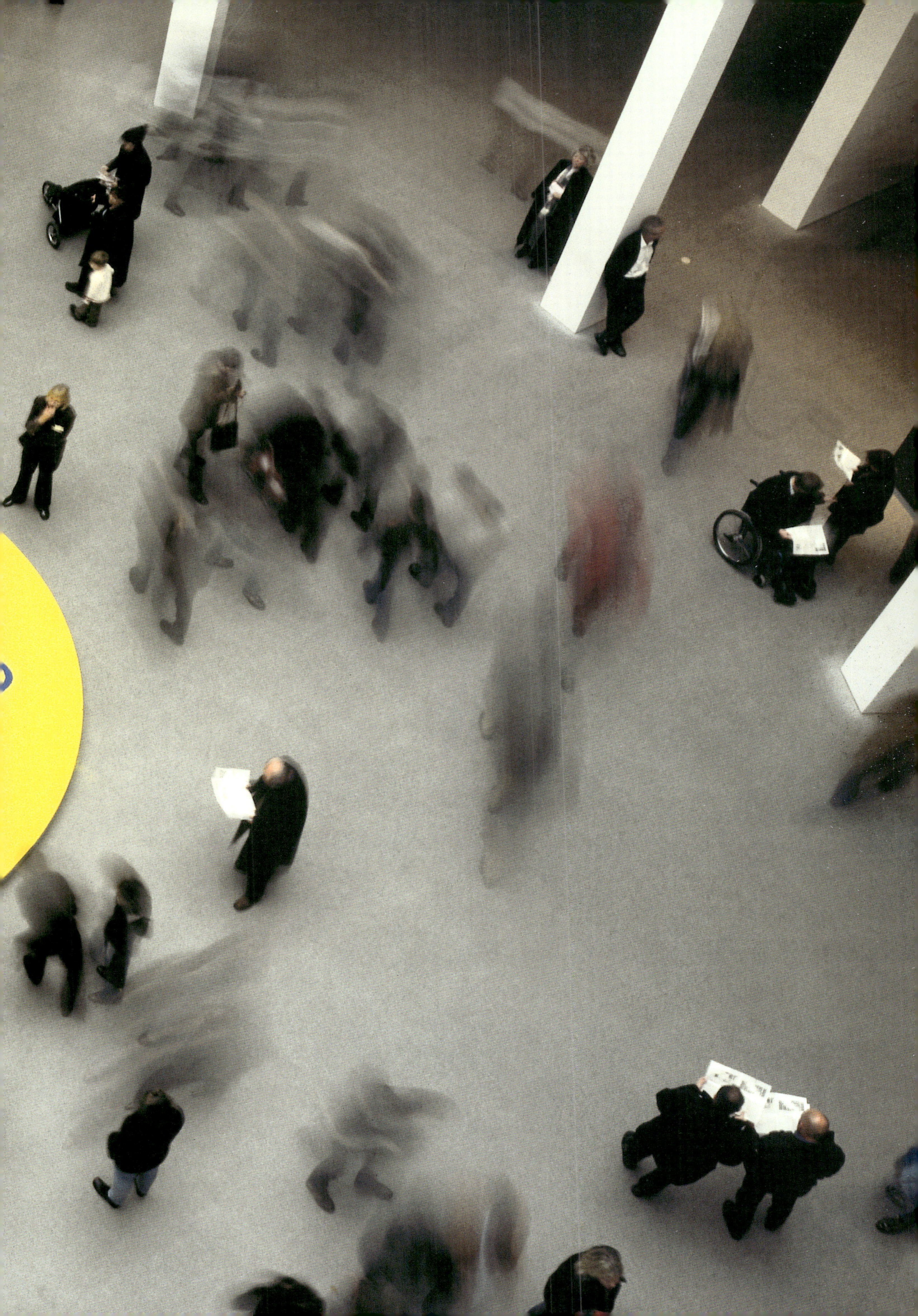

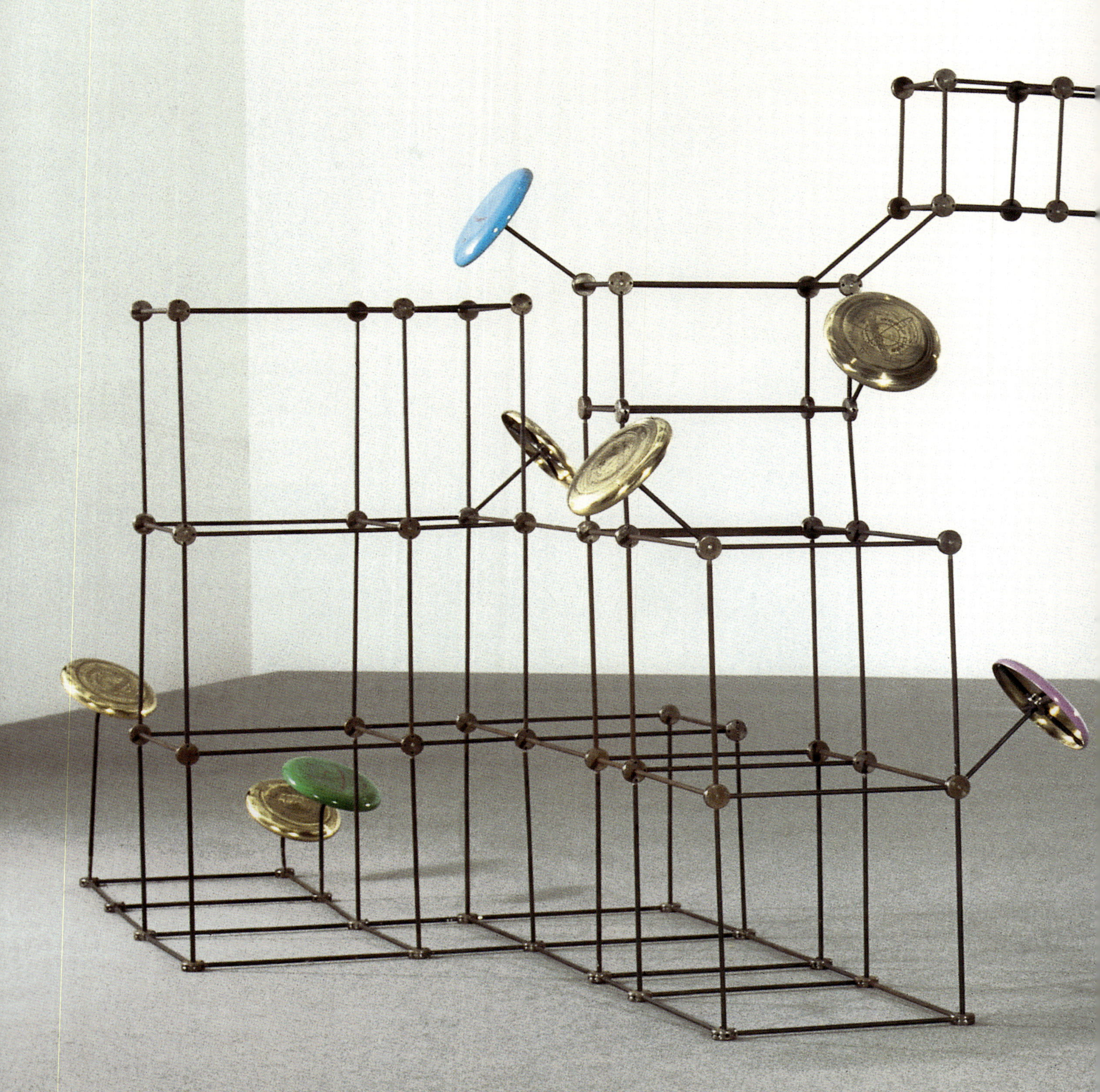

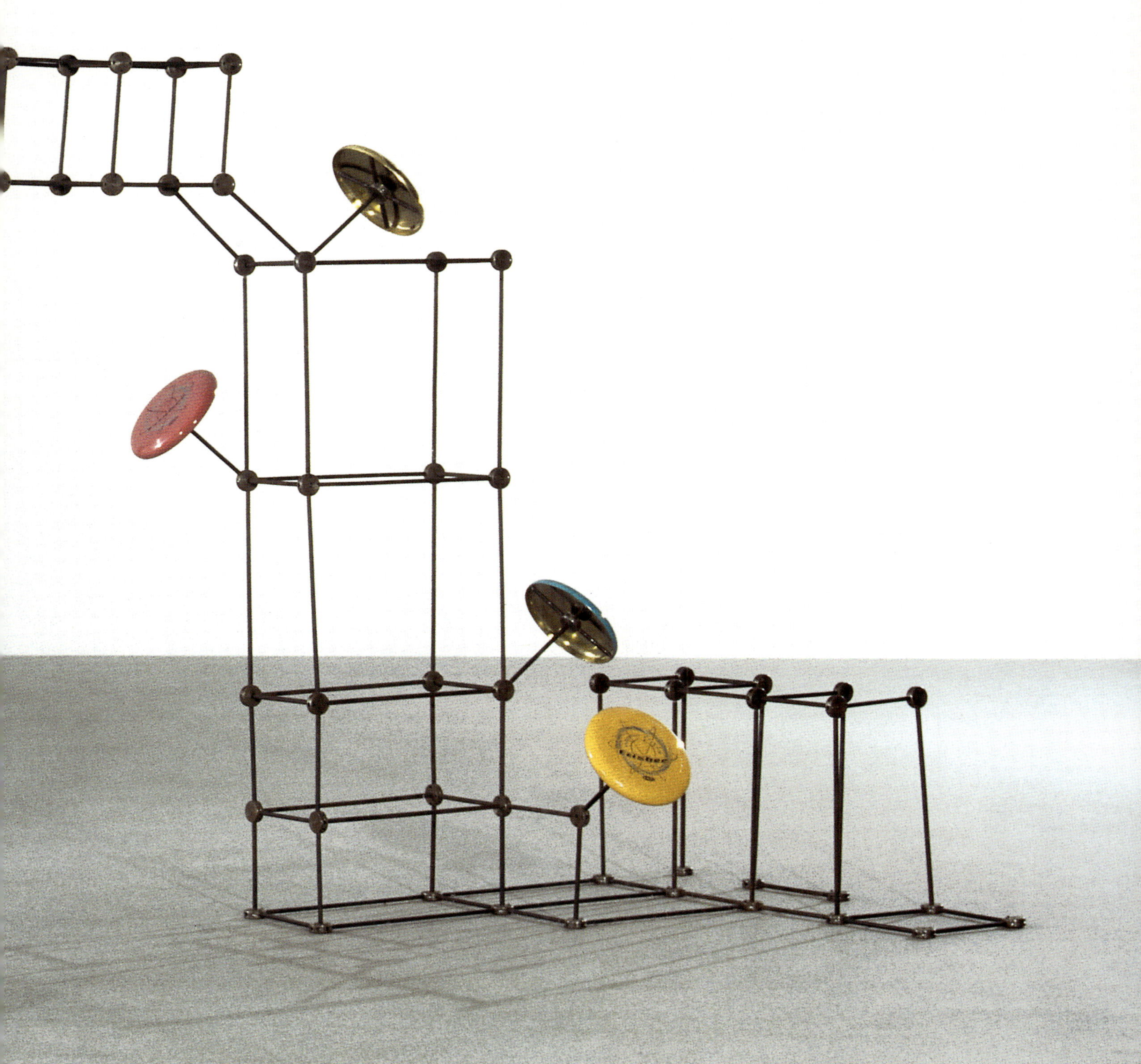

denn die zusammengekehrte Mischung einstmals konkreter Heilsmotive wird in einen Fluß geschüttet, so dass die Kräfte dann jeder Kreatur im Alltag zugänglich werden können. Weinstein hat ein als Markenprodukt eingetragenes Allerweltsobjekt mit der sakralen Form in Verbindung gebracht – ein gemeinhin verbotenes Spiel, definiert sich das Heilige (lat. sanctus, von sancire – umschließen) doch gerade dadurch, dass es vom profanen Bezirk abgetrennt ist (lat. fanum – Bezirk). Dies mag vom Gläubigen als Frevel, vom Gottsuchenden als frustrierende Doppeldeutigkeit wahrgenommen werden. Doch mit der mühevollen Herstellung einer vergänglichen Arbeit wird eine Analogie zur Condition humana jenseits geschützter Rückzugsorte geschaffen. Zugleich liegt in dieser deckungsgleichen Überlagerung zweier ursprünglich getrennter Territorien, das Potential zu einer mit Halluzinationen vergleichbaren Erfahrung – so, wie das Frisbee visionären Geistern tatsächlich als Gloriole über den Köpfen von Sportlern erscheinen mag, die mit ihren durchtrainierten Körpern für Momente den Traum eines endlosen Sommers und endloser Jugend erleben. Das Wissen um das, was aus pragmatischer Sicht ein Frisbee ist, wird in diesem Zustand überschritten, das sinnliche Sehen und das „innere" Sehen überlagern sich. Darüber hinaus signalisiert die aus Tausenden von „Pixeln" aufgebaute Struktur der Bodenarbeit, dass es sich hier um eine „virtuelle", um eine mögliche Wirklichkeit handelt, die – wie im Feld der digitalen Kultur immer wieder beschrieben – den Begriff der Identität auflöst, sind es doch nur Punkte, die, je nach Anzahl, einen höheren oder niedrigeren Realitätsgrad vorgeben.

Der Titel der Arbeit „Ed Headrick, Designer of the Modern Frisbee. Dies at 78" definiert das Werk als Denkmal der Erinnerung für den am 12. August 2002 verstorbenen Erfinder der „Fliegenden Untertassen". 1957 stand dieser vor der Herausforderung, einen neuen Verwendungszweck für eine ganze Lagerhalle voller Plastik zu finden, die ursprünglich für die Produktion von inzwischen aus der Mode gekommenen Hula-Hoop-Reifen erworben worden war. Headrick gelang ein echter „Wurf" mit der Erfindung des „Modern Frisbee", einem Produkt, dem er sich, wie aus einem Interview hervorgeht, mit Leib und Seele verschrieben hat. Ein knappes Jahr vor seinem Tod brachte er das Frisbee gar mit einer interessanten Vorstellung des Lebens nach dem Tod in Verbindung: „Wir sagten immer, das Frisbee ist wirklich eine Religion – wir nannten uns ‚Frisbyterianer'. Wenn wir sterben, kommen wir nicht ins Fegefeuer. Wir landen einfach auf einem Dach und bleiben dort liegen."

Eine Landung auf dem Dach? Ein goldener, ins profane Museum gefallener Heiligenschein? Ein vergängliches Monument für die Ewigkeit des Todes, ein Bild, das zwischen Erscheinen und Verschwinden changiert? – „Wir können", so Weinstein, „uns nur durch Halluzinationen den Grenzbereichen des Lebens nähern".

In der Vision entstehen unglaublich scharfe Bilder. CT

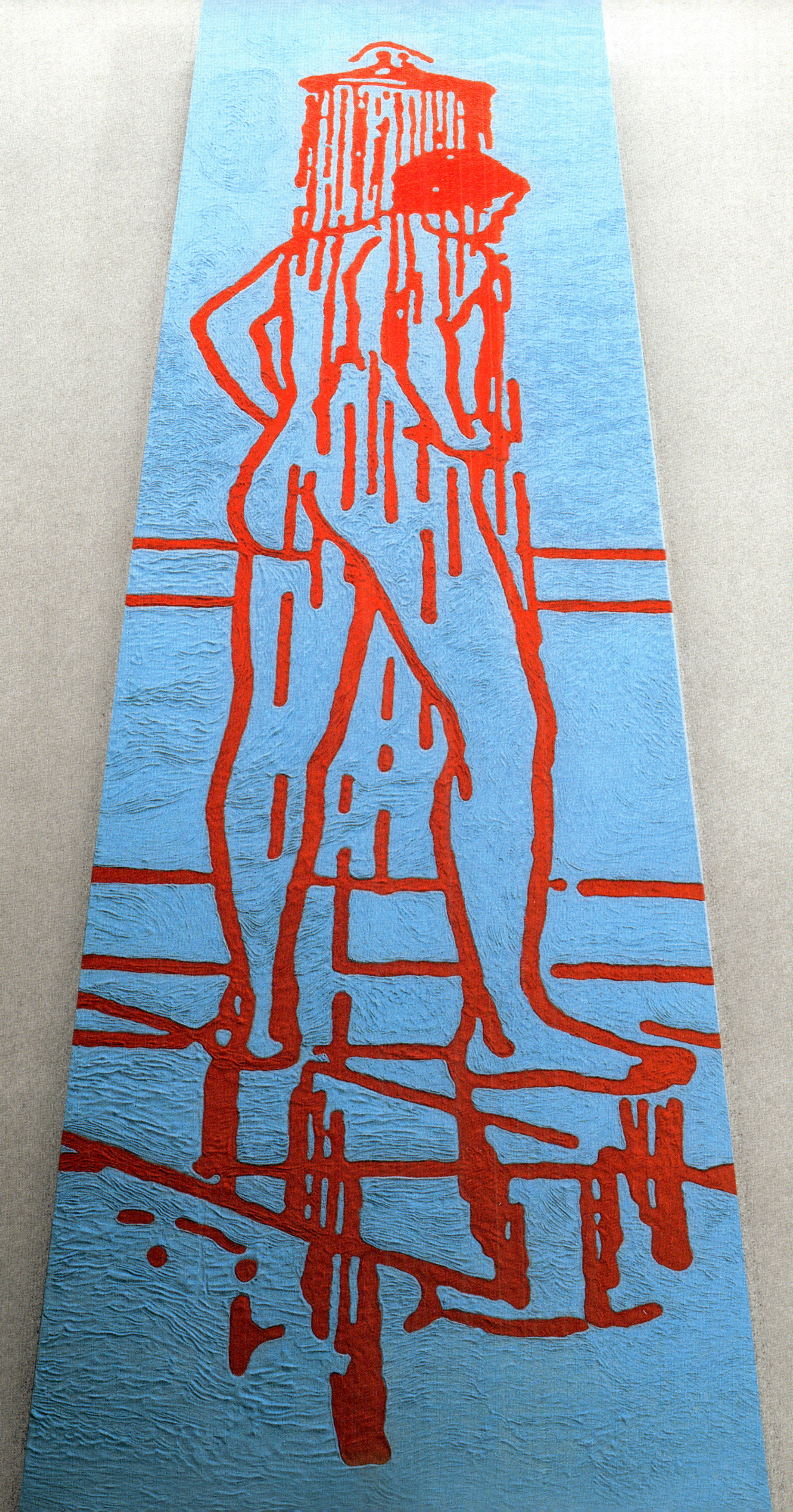

———————— empty vessels ————————

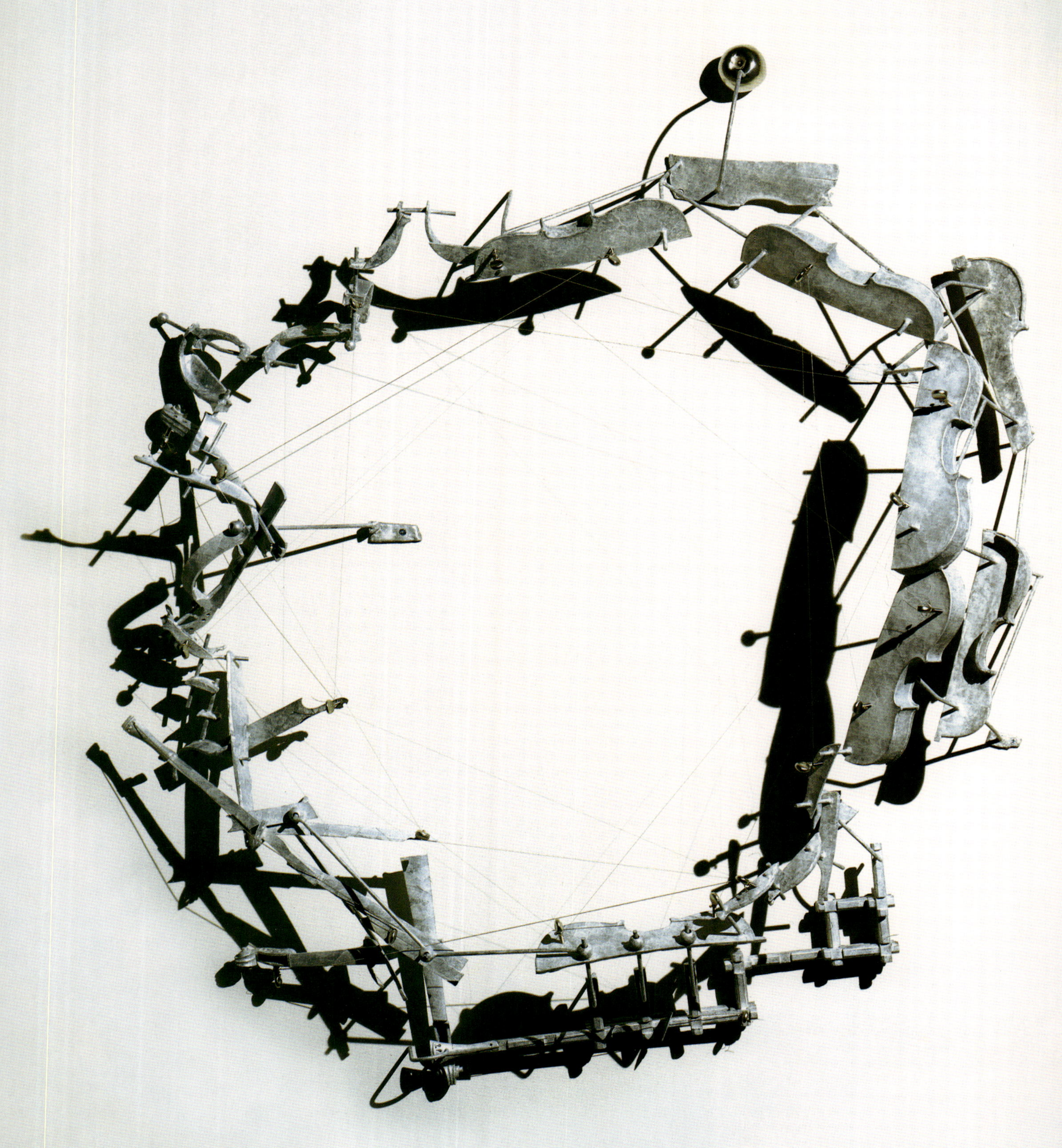

FROM THE BEAUTIFUL SOUND
OF EMPTY VESSELS

The myth of Sisyphus gives rise to a rigid portrayal of the futility of all human effort. But Sisyphus can also be viewed as the father of revolt. By contemplating his fate on his walk back down the hill, time after time, he is able to scorn the Gods. By so doing, he takes his fate into his own hands through the act of contemplation. "The absurd person, when he considers his anguish, ignores all graven images," according to Camus in "The Myth of Sisyphus". "The absurd person accepts (his fate) and his toil finds no end. (…) The fight against summits may fulfill a human life. We must perceive Sisyphus as a happy person." When Matthew Weinstein, in his bronze sculpture "Apples" (p. 4), brings together leafless gnarled branches and geometric DNA-like spiral structures into a putative unbroken circular upon which twelve painted apples are set like numbers on a clock face, he escorts us to Sisyphus' steep slope where the colossal rock repeatedly rolls back before he must roll it up the hill again.

In "Apples", of course, it is a potpourri of symbols of very differing descriptive world models that is being pushed uphill; the apple (the paradise myth), the double helix (the conquest of nature over culture). Perhaps these models disqualify each other. Perhaps they assist each other in the creation of meaning as each of their individual blueprints cannot single-handedly answer all of the questions that they inherently hold.

There's something strangely joyful in Weinstein's melancholic circle of dying branches. Perhaps his aesthetic glee stems from his found ability to contemplate and thus take control of overbearing cultural norms through the act of representation. Like Camus' Sisyphus, in Weinstein's work, power is scorned through identification. Like the revelers in Mexico's "Day of the Dead", who dress as death in order to exhibit their lack of fear, Weinstein is identifying the unconquerable enemy (the forces of history that cannot be changed, as well as the physical inevitabilities that cannot be avoided) in order to preserve his human dignity.

In the bronze sculpture "My Name is Asher Lev" (p. 34), there arises an examination of utopia and reality, history and the concrete present, "the own" and the "foreign", "the outdated" and the "current". The never ending cycle of culture and renewal is here fashioned out of cast bronze violin fragments, which are welded into a circle and then bound by a spider web of violin strings, strung tight with chrome tuners, so that a new chaotic instrument is formed.

The title of the sculpture is borrowed from the novel of the same name by Chaim Potok. In this novel, a Brooklyn-bred boy and his Hasidic family and community enter into conflict because of the boy's desire to become an artist. The young Asher Lev cannot carry on with the demanding and all-embracing

VOM SCHÖNEN KLANG
LEERER GEFÄSSE

Der mythische Bericht von Sisyphos liefert ein Bild für die Vergeblichkeit allen menschlichen Tuns. Aber Sisyphos kann auch als Vater der Revolte angerufen werden, der die gottgewollte ewige Verdammnis verachtet und sein Schicksal selbst in die Hand nimmt, indem er darüber reflektiert. „Der absurde Mensch lässt, wenn er seine Qual bedenkt", so Camus in „Der Mythos des Sisyphos", „alle Götzenbilder schweigen. [...] Der absurde Mensch sagt ja [zu seinem Schicksal] und seine Anstrengung hört nicht mehr auf. [...] Der Kampf gegen Gipfel vermag ein Menschenleben auszufüllen. Wir müssen uns Sisyphos als glücklichen Menschen vorstellen."

Wenn der im „Big Apple" New York arbeitende Matthew Weinstein in seiner Bronzeskulptur „Apples" (S. 4) Abformungen blattloser Zweige und geometrische, an DNS-Spiralen erinnernde Strukturen zu einer vermeintlich bruchlosen Kreisform zusammenfügt, auf der zwölf farbig bemalte Äpfel wie Zahlen auf dem runden Zifferblatt einer Uhr erscheinen, führt er uns in den steilen Hang des Sisyphos, an dem der kolossale Felsbrocken immer wieder hinabrollt und vom Unermüdlichen stets aufs Neue hinaufbewegt wird. Hier werden anstelle des Felsens freilich gewichtige Elemente verschiedenster Erklärungsmodelle der Welt gestemmt: Der Apfel (Paradiesgeschichte), Zweige (Natur) und DNS-Kette (Wissenschaft). Die mit diesen Elementen verbundenen Modelle disqualifizieren sich gegenseitig und ergänzen sich zugleich. Doch auch ihr Miteinander kann die vom Leben aufgeworfenen Fragen nicht vollständig beantworten.

Indem Weinstein mit Fragmenten arbeitet, schreibt er sich in den Lauf der ihm überlieferten Geschichte ein. Wie Camus' Sisyphos bestätigt er mit der wiederholten Verwendung jedes Versatzstückes seine Reflexion über die Autorität kultureller Normen – und gewinnt dadurch an Freiheit. Den am Totensonntag in Mexiko feiernden Menschen vergleichbar, die sich als Tod verkleiden, um ihr Bewusstsein gegenüber dieser Bedrohung zu signalisieren, identifiziert auch Weinstein die nicht beherrschbaren Kräfte (der Geschichte ebenso wie die unabwendbaren Bedingungen, die der Körper stellt), um seine Würde als Mensch zu schützen.

In „Mein Name ist Asher Lev" (S. 34) findet ebenfalls eine Befragung von Utopie und Wirklichkeit, Geschichte und konkreter Gegenwart, von „eigenen" und „fremden", „überholten" und „aktuellen" Elementen statt. Der Kreislauf aus Zerstörung und Neubeginn wird hier aus Bronzeabformungen von Violinenbruchstücken und dem „Spinnennetz" bizarr gespannter Saiten gebildet. Der Titel der Skulptur ist Chaim Potoks gleichnamigem Roman entliehen. Darin wird die Geschichte eines in der Geborgenheit einer chassidischen Familie in Brooklyn aufwachsenden Jungen beschrieben, der Künstler werden möchte

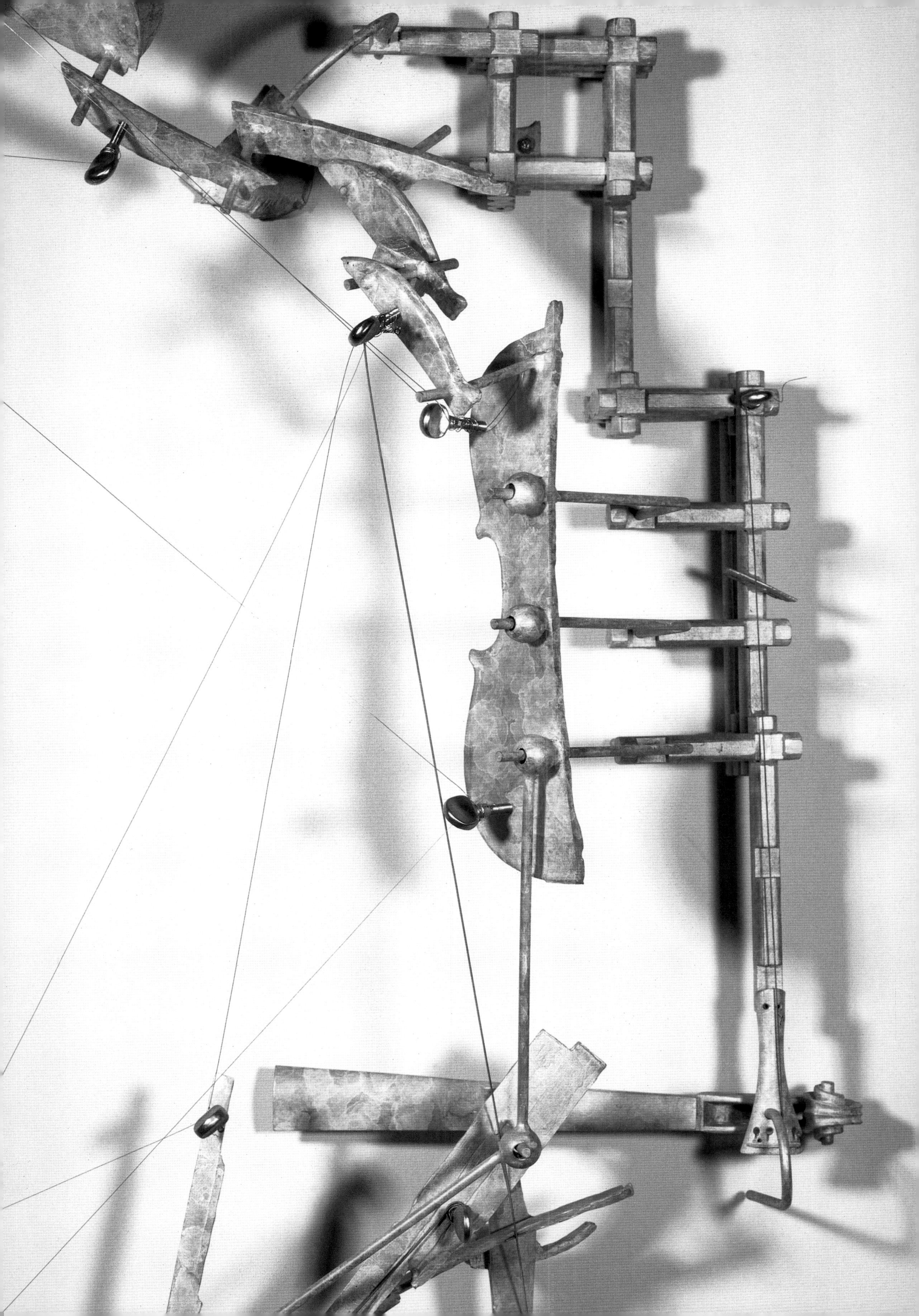

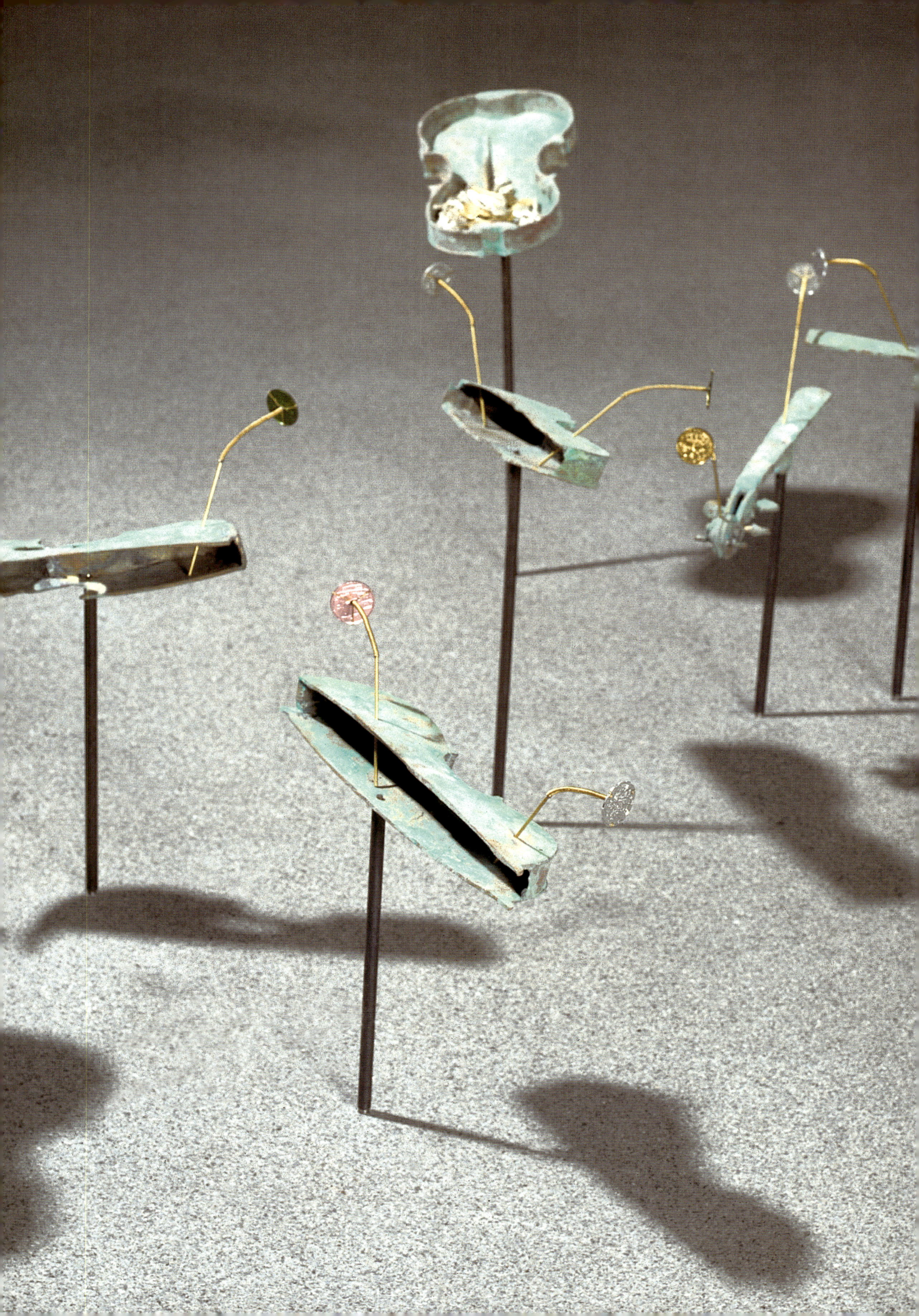

traditions of his immediate sphere, as its germane set of laws collide with his
own desires. The novel is a compelling enquiry into the power of aesthetic modi
operandi, which is relevant for Weinstein as well. Does the rejection of one
confirm that its replacement is any more meaningful? Are there "Universal Pictures"
of perceived reality that can be universally understood, even if not accepted?
Or are artists preoccupied with "empty vessels", with symbols, ideas and signs that
create promises that cannot be put into force, as they are only the voluble
arrangements of individuals which can never be a rational argument for all?
Weinstein compares this sculpture to the tale of the goose that laid the golden egg.
The goose is an empty vessel, no golden eggs could be found inside it
when it was butchered. The violin has no music inside it. The sculpture looks as
if the violins were shattered in order to find the music inside. But in his
desire for music, Weinstein reassembles the violins into a multi-stringed mutation
of the source. So something new is made, perhaps a new paradigm for music.
"Splashes of Vo-Vomit" (p. 42) is an empty vessel as well, a worn out
old shoe hyper-realistically cast in bronze. But how empty is the furrowed reality
of the footwear? Is it garbage or is there, in every mark and crease,
a memory of an individually lived life that deserves immortality in bronze.
A verse from Arthur Rimbaud's poem, "The Drunken Boat", has been carefully
engraved onto the bronze. To read it you must kneel down before the boot,
which sits forlornly on the floor. You must put your face close to the floor and
crawl in a circle around the boot to read the lines that spiral around
its exterior. In order to examine this object, you are forced to show humility to a
vanished and anonymous human presence.
In "The Drunken Boat", the human body is compared to a boat that, without
a rudder or an anchor, without the aid of civilization and convention, is tossed
about in the ocean. The flushing out of all that is bodily and the freedom
that accompanies this is described by the poet as "sweeter than the flesh of sour
apples", as it leads to an authentic encounter with the elements. Concurrently,
the journey is the cause of horror, pain and, if rigorously carried through, leads
to death. An alternative to this unconditional self-abandonment
towards a potential emptiness is that which Weinstein develops in his works.
They are a direct expression of the search for rapprochement and balance. They
are a picture puzzle of the extreme: the search for meaning in the
arbitrary and vicious circle of sundry assurances, out of which we can use, each
time, only fragments. His work is a constructive countering through
continually and persistently questioning the world and the power of its employed
symbols. The artist builds on the broad sound of direct communication. CT

und dadurch in Konflikt mit seinem direkten Umfeld gerät. Die ihm vermittelten
Regeln kollidieren mit seiner eigenen Wahrnehmung. Daraus resultiert die
auch für Weinstein gültige Frage nach Wirkung und Bedeutung ästhetischer
Formeln in der Kunst. Bestätigt die Ablehnung der Einen gerade, dass ihre
Aussage für Andere sinnvoller Ausdruck mit der Welt sein kann? Gibt es
„Universal Pictures", die überall verstanden, wenn auch nicht akzeptiert werden?
Oder beschäftigen sich Künstler mit „leeren Gefäßen", mit Symbolen,
Zeichen und Kompositionen, Versprechungen, die nie in Kraft treten können,
weil es sich nur um kommunikative Vereinbarungen Einzelner handelt, die
niemals eine sinnvolle Ordnung für Alle sein können?
Weinstein zieht eine Verbindung zwischen dieser Skulptur und dem Märchen
„Die Gans, die goldene Eier legt". In der sich als vergeblich erweisenden Hoffnung,
einen Goldklumpen im Bauch des Tieres zu finden, wurde die Gans
geschlachtet. Der Vergleich suggeriert, dass auch die hohlen Klangkörper der
Violinen auf der Suche nach Musik zerschlagen worden sind. Doch aus
den Fragmenten wurde auch ein neues Instrument gebaut, das zu einem neuen
Paradigma für Musik werden kann.
Auch „Splashes of Vo-Vomit" (S. 42) ist ein leeres Gefäß, ein abgetragener Schuh.
Wie „leer" aber ist die runzlige Wirklichkeit des Schuhwerks wirklich?
Ist es ein überaltertes Wegwerfprodukt oder aber mit jeder Falte ein Zeichen
individuell gelebten Lebens, das bewahrenden Schutz verdient? Eine Verewigung in
Bronze? Auf der Außenseite der Skulptur hat Weinstein einen Vers aus Arthur
Rimbauds Gedicht „Das trunkene Schiff" eingraviert. Um die spiralförmig
verlaufenden Worte zu entziffern, muss man sich zu diesem wie Strandgut am
Boden stehenden Schuh niederknien. Nur in dieser demütigen Haltung, nur,
wenn man die fast Schwindel erregenden Lesebewegung akzeptiert, kann man
dieses Zeugnis einer verschwundenen menschlichen Existenz kennen lernen.
In der Aufschrift wird der menschliche Körper einem Boot verglichen, das ohne
Ruder, ohne Anker, ohne Hilfsmittel von Zivilisation und Konvention, im
Wasser treibt. Das Auswaschen alles Körperlichen, die damit entstehende Freiheit
wird „süßer als das Fleisch saurer Äpfel" beschrieben, denn sie führt zur
unverstellten Begegnung mit den Elementen. Zugleich ist diese Reise Ursache von
Schrecken, Schmerzen, und, wird sie konsequent betrieben, führt sie zum Tod.
Eine Alternative zu dieser bedingungslosen Selbstaufgabe in eine mögliche Leere
hinein entwickelt Weinstein mit seinen Werken. Sie sind direkter Ausdruck
einer Suche nach Verständigung und Balance. Dem Vexierspiel der Extreme, dem
Dilemma zwischen Sinn und Beliebigkeit, dem Teufelskreis der verschiedenen
Heilsversprechen, tritt er konstruktiv entgegen, indem er die Welt und die Kraft
der in ihr benutzten Symbole mit Beharrlichkeit immer wieder neu
in Frage stellt. Er baut auf den vollen Laut der direkten Kommunikation. CT

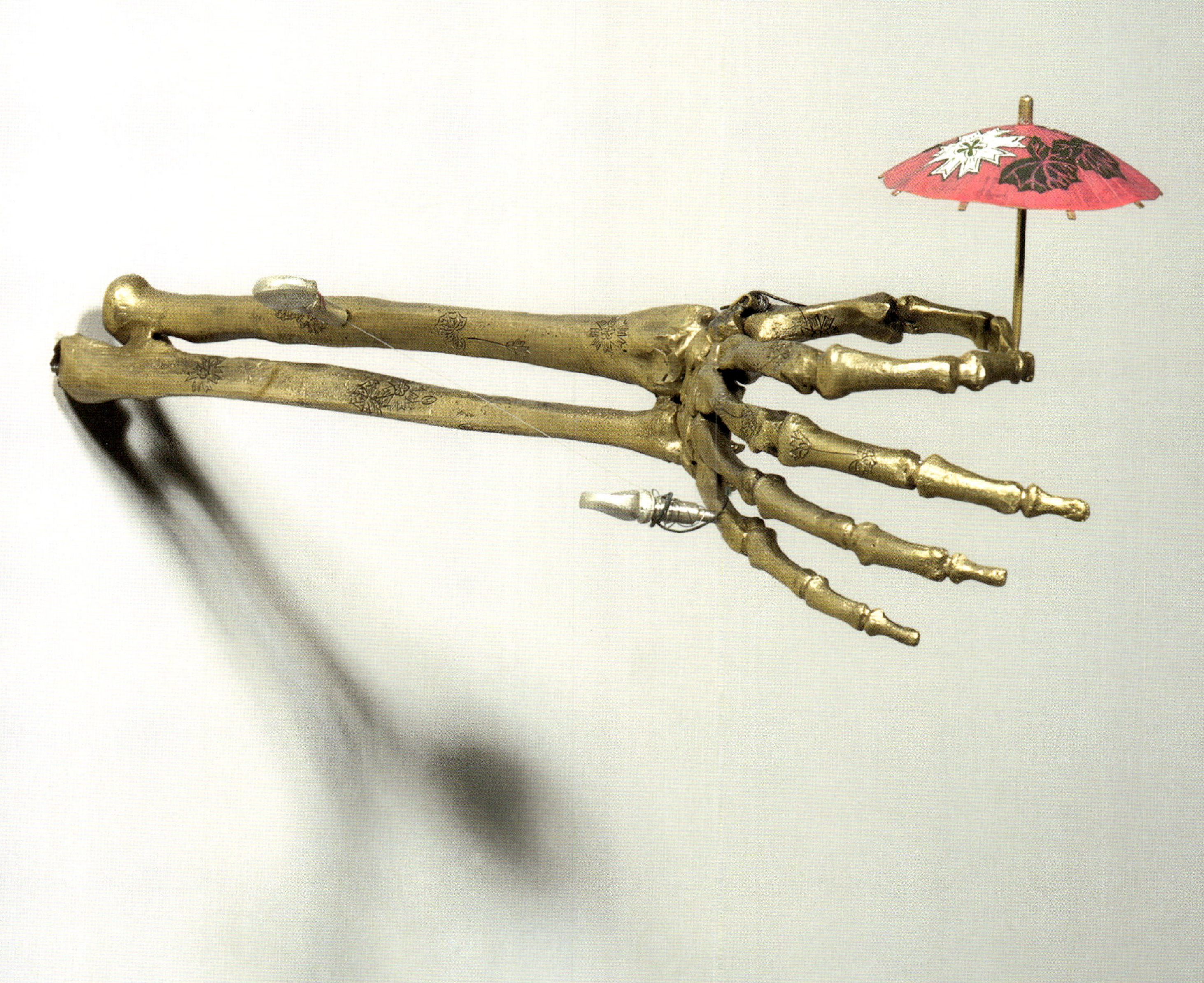

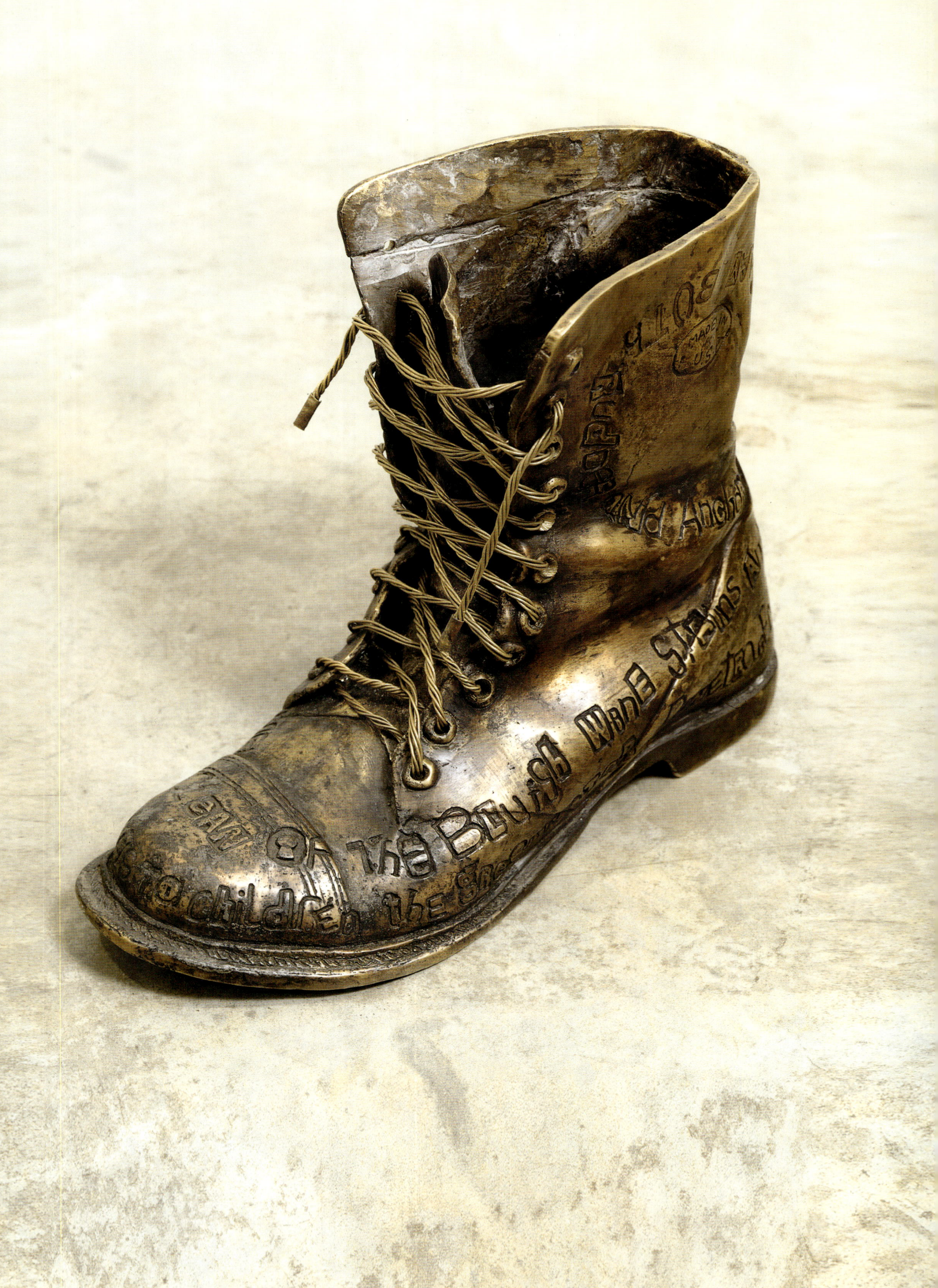

“SWEETER THAN THE FLESH
OF SOUR APPLES TO CHILDREN,
THE GREEN WATER
PENETRATED MY PINEWOOD HULL
AND WASHED ME CLEAN
OF THE BLUISH WINESTAINS AND
THE SPLASHES OF VOMIT,
CARRYING AWAY
BOTH RUDDER AND ANCHOR.”

Quoted from Arthur Rimbaud: The Drunken Boat

„VIEL SÜSSER ALS DER HERBEN
ÄPFEL FLEISCH DEM KINDE,
DURCHDRANG MICH GRÜNES NASS,
WUSCH BLAUEN WEIN UND
DRECK HINAB VON DES BESPIENEN
SCHIFFES TANNENRINDE
UND RISS MIR DAS STEUER MITSAMT
DEM ANKER WEG.“

Aus Arthur Rimbaud: Das trunkene Schiff

———————— exchange and offering ————————

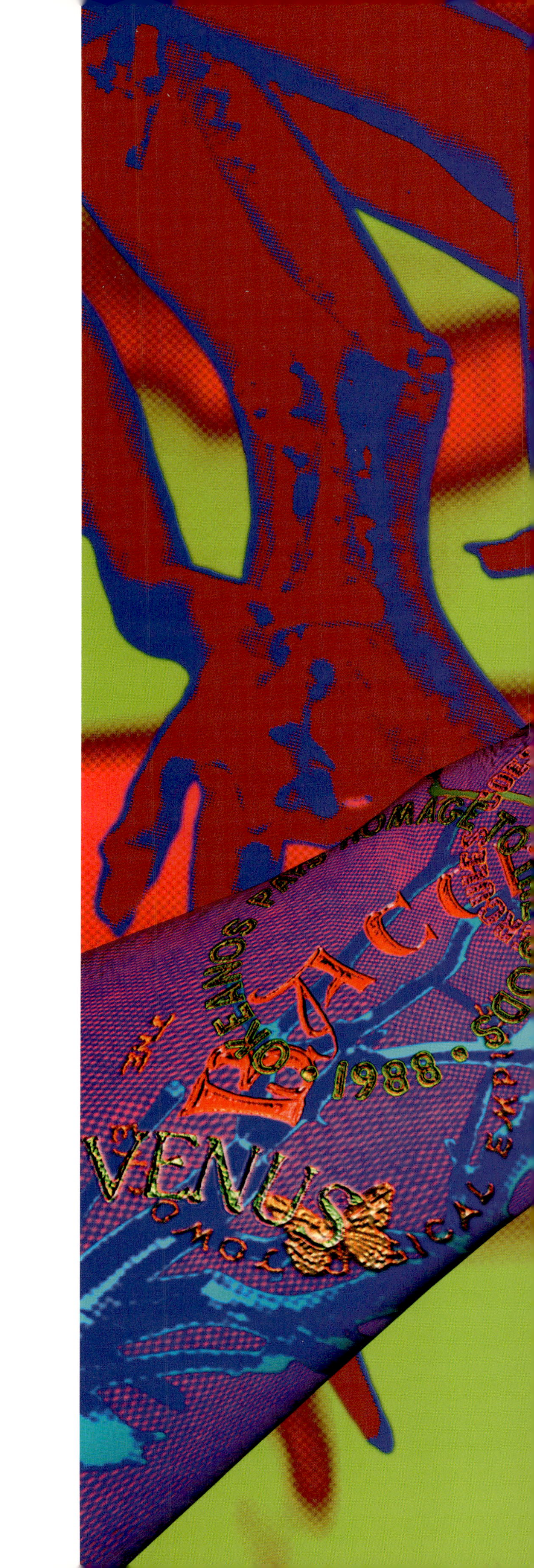
ONE HOMAGES PAYS HOMAGE
JACE
VENUS
1988
LOGICAL EXPLODE

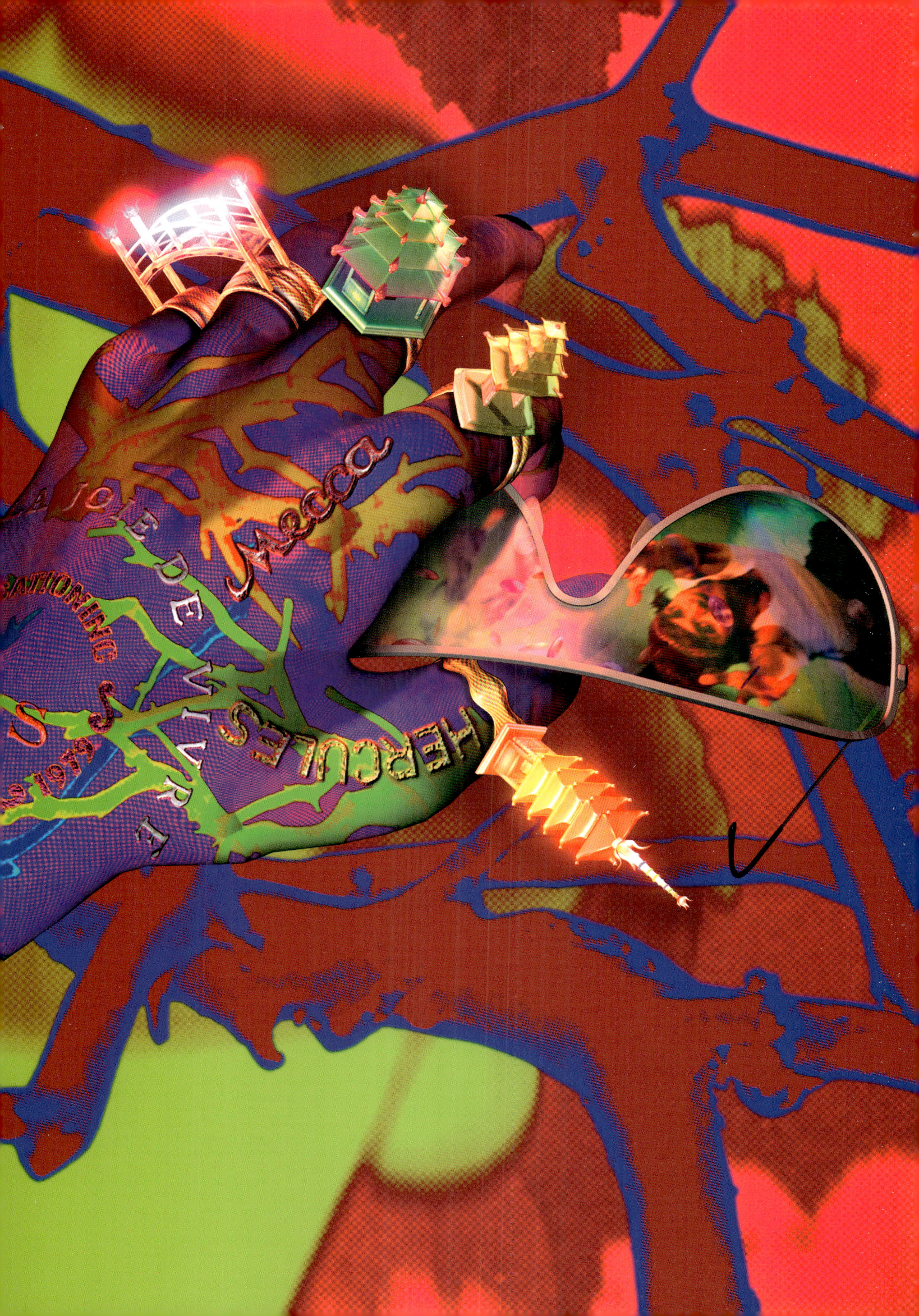

Mecca
LA JOIE DE VIVRE
HERCULES

DIE GESCHÜTZE DER WARENWELT

Sonnenbrillen, Labels, Talismane und Tattoos – moderne Krieger sind bis zum Anschlag mit ästhetischen Insignien bewaffnet. Ihre zweite Haut strahlt im kalten Glanz der heißen Produkte, sie wehrt den intimen Blick ab und fordert doch zur Frage nach dem davon Verborgenen heraus. In „Branches" (S. 46/47) inkarnieren sich in Form von mäandernden Tätowierungen Archetypen jeder Art von Gesellschaft auf der vom Astwerk der Natur durchfurchten Hand: Die Schriftzüge „Herkules" und „Venus" signalisieren das Männliche, das Weibliche, dem Pilger steht sein „Mekka" vor Augen, dem Glücksritter sein „Joie de Vivre". Das Bild ist auf die große Bahn eines halbtransparenten Seidenstoffs gedruckt, die Segel für die Einschiffung nach Kythera sind gehisst. Denn worauf, wenn nicht auf elysische Gefilde und den endlosen Weg dorthin, verweisen die unter Schmerzen, Kosten, Lust erworbenen Zeichen des Panzers? Das Allover des goldenen Stacheldrahts (S. 50/51) ist die Rüstung des Verletzlichen. Die Geschütze der Warenwelt dringen, auf der Haut getragen, in den Stoffwechsel des Körpers ein. Die Tiefe der Welt liegt auf der Haut. Auf der Haut beginnt der Kult um die Oberfläche, und die Haut ist der Nabel zu Vergnügen und Schmerz, die sich in die Tiefe des Körpers einsenken. Begehren und Konsum gehen dabei nicht im einfachen Tausch auf, denn Gerechtigkeit im Geben und Nehmen wird nur empfunden, wenn den entzauberten, käuflichen Produkten im täglichen Gebrauch die Sprache sakraler Objekte aufgehext wird. Durch diese Manipulation werden die Objekte zum apotropäischen Fetisch. Schall und Rauch der Warenwelt stehen an der Pforte zur erträumten Insel der Glückseligkeit. Um vergleichbare Verwandlungen geht es auch im monumentalen Deckenbild „Dhalgren" (S. 20/21). Anstelle von Göttern und Engeln bewohnen hier „beautiful people" die himmlische Sphäre. Anstelle von Manna fallen Falschmünzen herab, jene farbenprächtige Taler, die am Fastnachtsdienstag in New Orleans über die Besucher geworfen werden, um wahren Goldsegen zu suggerieren. Die Taler sind mit mythologischen Beschriftungen versehen, Worte, die ebenfalls in „Branches" aufgenommen wurden. Im Illusionismus von „Dhalgren" wird der kontinuierliche Transfer und die Verwandlung von Ideen, Wünschen und Vorstellungen sichtbar gemacht. Die Figuren des Bildes schauen auf uns herab. Suchen sie unsere Teilnahme am Spiel, dessen Regeln wir selbst aufbauen? Träumen. In „Excessive Dreaming" (S. 54/55) sind die bronzenen Abformungen einer Tempelminiatur und eines menschlichen Ohres mit einem Draht verbunden. Das realistisch große Ohr ist die Verkleinerung eines Modells für Akupunkteure, auf dem alle für eine Behandlung bekannten Punkte markiert sind. Vom Arzt des Dalai Lama – wer hätte einen verheißungsvolleren Mediziner finden können? – ließ Weinstein nun Nadeln an jenen Stellen setzen, die zur Therapie exzessiver

THE ARTILLERY OF THE
PRODUCT WORLD

Sunglasses, labels, talismans and tattoos. The modern warrior is armed to the hilt
with aesthetic symbols. This second skin radiates with the cool glow of
hot products that defend the skin beneath while providing enticement to touch
or destroy the human warmth within. In "Branches" (p. 46/47), societal
archetypes are incarnated in the form of meandering tattoos on a gigantic
computer generated image of a hand. The tattoos "Hercules" and "Venus" stand
for masculinity and femininity. The pilgrim imagines his "Mecca", while
the adventurer fulfils his "Joie de Vivre". The naturalist can contemplate the
breadth of his "Entomological Empire".

"Branches" takes the form of a sixteen foot square panel of digitally dyed
Chinese silk. It is a sail hoisted for the embarkation to Cythera, for where else do
the medals for valor gain us admittance to? They are won through pain,
expense and lust. They are like a trail of breadcrumbs leading to the
Elysian fields. These symbolic objects are the artillery of the product world. The
world's depth lies on the surface of the body. The skin is the umbilicus
to amusement and pain, both of which descend into the depths of the corpus.
Desire and consumption. Not an equal exchange. The sense of equanimity
can only be obtained between the two impulses when the de-mystified
purchasable product is ensconced within the language of the sacred object.
The myth of the sacred object is that it fulfils; it satisfies desire on a holistic level.
Through this manipulation, the objects will morph into apotropaic fetishes.
The rigorous superficiality of the product world stands at the gate to the bliss we
attempt to obtain.

In another giant sail, "Fall III" (p. 50/51), an all over pattern of golden barbed
wire blocks a deeper layer of atmospheric abstraction. This deeper
layer is red, warm and off limits. Glorified aggression vs. aesthetically imbued
vulnerability. The armour over the skin.

Weinstein points out that the slogans advertised on the pieces "Branches" (p. 46/67)
and "Continental Drift" (p. 82/83) come from Mardi Gras doubloon
(shiny fake coins, tossed around during Mardi Gras in New Orleans, bearing the
mythological mascots of various social organizations) picked up off
the floor of a nightclub by the artist in a random order. Are we in the world of
sense or nonsense? Overhead is a fourth sail, "Dhalgren" (p. 20/21).

Dyed into a monumental expanse of silk are images of "the beautiful people"
flying around in a computer generated Tiepolo-like miasma. They are chasing
the coins and catching Frisbees. Is this a game with rules or unbridled chaos?
They look down at us. Do they want us to play or have we angered them?

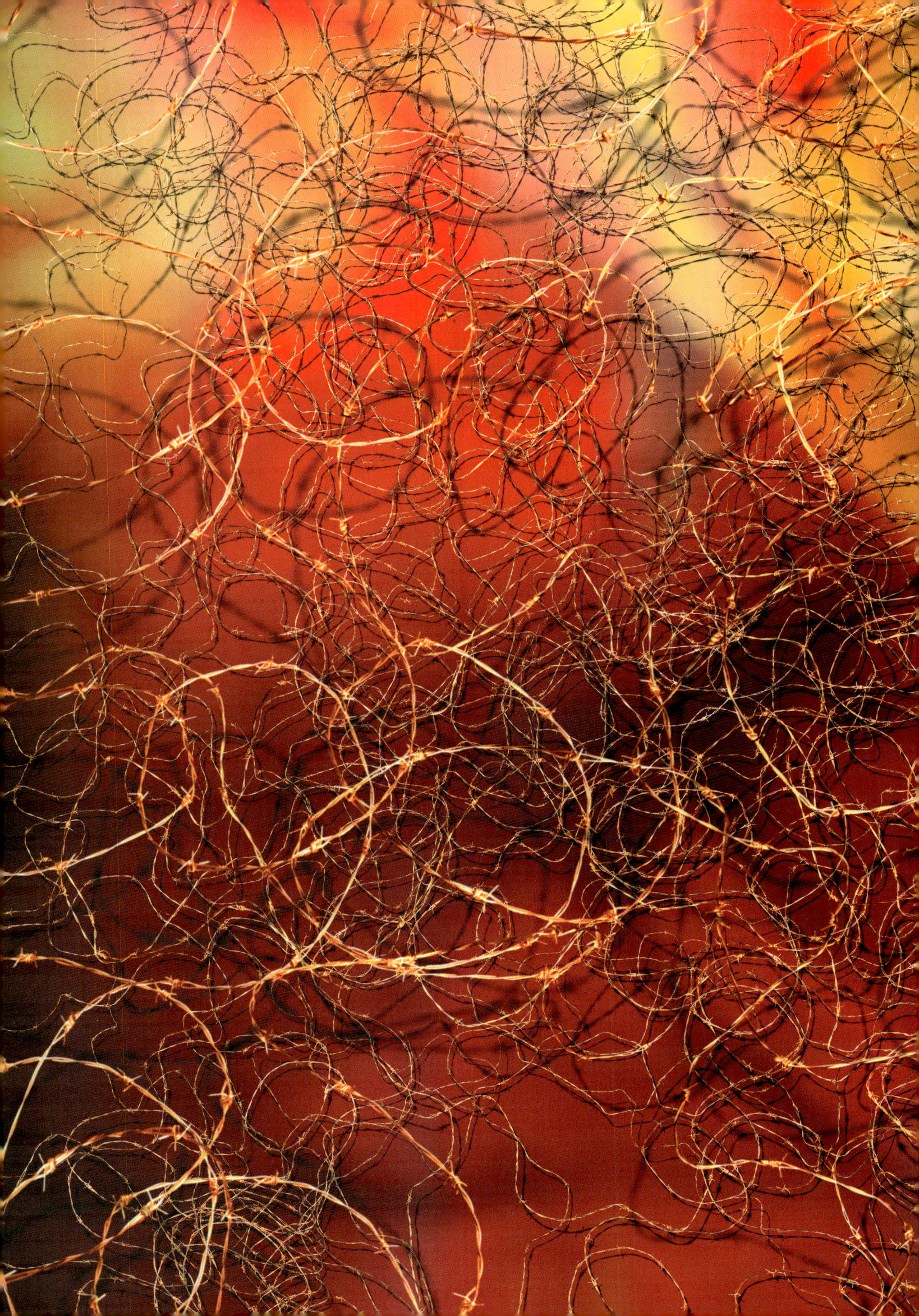

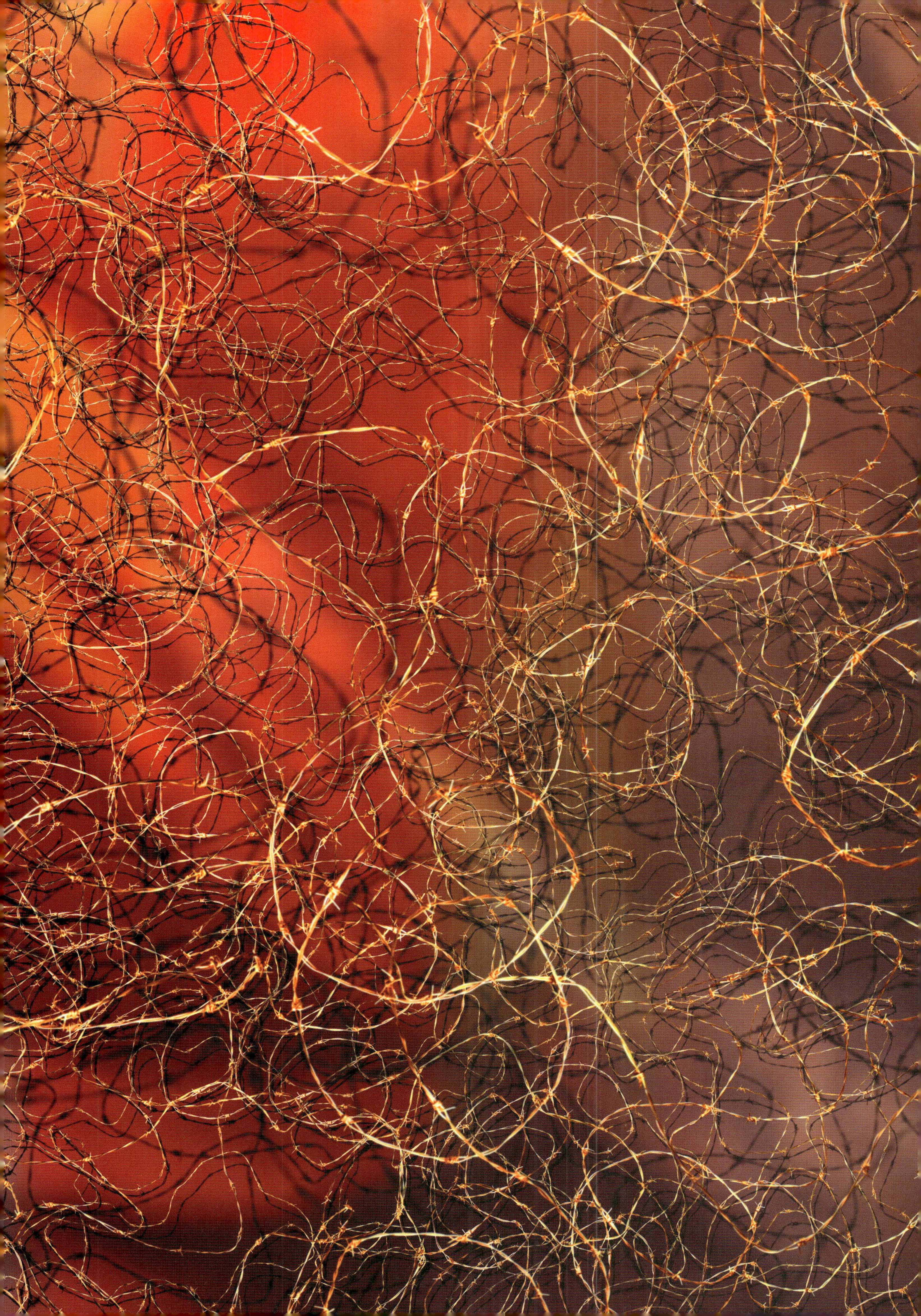

Träume angezeigt sind, eine Behandlung, die sich der Künstler für die mit Traum und Vision verdrehten Wahrnehmungen von Wirklichkeit zu wünschen scheint. Allerdings wirft er mit dem Werk insgesamt die Frage auf, ob der von Träumen verblendete Mensch die Botschaft der Nadeln in der gebotenen Deutlichkeit wahrnehmen kann, denn das Ohr ist über einen Draht mit dem Tempel verbunden, der sich somit als weiterer „Gesprächsteilnehmer" einschaltet. Vergleichbare Mini-Repliken asiatischer Sakralarchitektur, eigentlich Gefäße für Reliquien, werden in vielen Asia-Geschäften des Westens als Glücksbringer (materialisiertes Bild für einen Glauben und zugleich Tand) angeboten und finden reichlichen Absatz. Der daran anschließende Draht verdeutlicht nicht nur, dass der Tempel eine wie auch immer geartete Bedeutung kommuniziert, sondern erinnert zugleich an die stupide oder überaus anspruchsvolle Musik, die Menschen via Walkman auf sich einprasseln lassen während sie sich gleichzeitig anderen Tätigkeiten widmen. Die Skulptur ist das „Porträt" eines modernen Städters, der mit Musik und Informationen bombardiert wird, während er sich auf dem Handy über die umfassende Wirkung von Yoga unterhält, dabei eine Zigarette raucht und die wirbelnde Welt durch die pinkfarbenen Gläser seiner Sonnenbrillen anschaut. Für ihn ist Überstimulation die Basis jeder Erfahrung. Sein Mund, seine Augen, seine Ohren öffnen sich im Laufe des Tages weiter und weiter, bis er eine Pille nimmt und schläft.

Um das konzentrierte Lauschen auf eine Aussage, die gleichsam nur im Flüsterton formuliert wird, geht es in „Whisper" (S. 57). Keine aufgeblasene Wirklichkeit ist hier zu sehen, kein Abrakadabra der in Waren inkarnierten Hirngespinste, keine Symbole, sondern eine intime Geste, die zwei Menschen in unmittelbarer Körperlichkeit miteinander in Verbindung treten lässt. Gezeigt ist der unvermittelte und natürliche Kern von Kommunikation jenseits der mit Magie überladenen Maske, die Verletzlichkeit und Unsicherheit kaschiert. Hier wird die Distanz zwischen individuell vorgestellter und tatsächlicher Wirklichkeit in der Gegenwart des Ereignisses aufgelöst. Direkte Kommunikation ist das Paradigma für Gegenwart. Ihre Gültigkeit lässt allenfalls eine Stellungnahme zu, nachdem die Botschaft in Kraft getreten ist. In Weinsteins Bild wird die Handlung nicht genauer spezifiziert, kein Ort wird angedeutet, Gesten, Mimik, die Augen sind nicht zu sehen, damit entfällt visuelle Reizüberflutung. Findet hier im warmen Licht eine gefährliche oder eine bezaubernd innige Szene statt? Das Bild verlangt die volle Aufmerksamkeit für die Bedeutung der Sprache jenseits vorgestanzter Bilder. Es ist ein Universal Picture für Kommunikation mit allem Risiko. Der Ausschnitt lässt hoffen, dass hier Begehren keine Versachlichung durch Konsum findet, nicht Immaterielles (Worte) durch Materielles unzufriedenstellend getauscht wird, sondern das gerechte gemeinsame Genießen stattfindet. Nur die Gabe der Liebe macht den Tausch für beide Seiten symmetrisch. CT

Dreaming. In "Excessive Dreaming" (p. 54/55), sterling silver reproductions of a miniature temple and a human ear are connected by a silver walkman headphone. The realistic ear is actually cast from an acupuncture teaching device in which all of the known points for a treatment are located. The silver temple is a repoussé replica of a mini model of an unidentified piece of Chinese religious architecture. The original is sold as a lucky trinket in New York's Chinatown. Like porcelain statues of Jesus or plastic Buddhas it is an example of the reification of belief into kitsch. Weinstein requested the Dalai Lama's acupuncturist (who could have found a more promising physician?) to position the needles on the points on the silver ear indicated for the treatment of "Excessive Dreaming", a fitting choice of malady for Weinstein for whom reality seems to be a constantly morphing hallucination. But can the dream-blinded individual discern the message of the needles when he is simultaneously listening to the information emitted from the temple? This piece is a "portrait" of a modern urbanite. He is bombarded with music and information while talking on his cell phone about the benefits of Yoga, while smoking a cigarette and gazing out at the swirling world through pink sunglasses. For him, over-stimulation is only the base level of sensorial experience. His mouth, eyes and ears are opened up wider and wider during the course of the day until he takes a pill to fall asleep. Straining one's ears to pick up a bat's squeak of communication is the content of "Whisper II" (p. 57). Here there is no inflated reality, no abracadabra of incarnated fantasies through products and no symbols. Rather, an intimate gesture that unites two people is represented. The nucleus of communication is shown. A mouth and an ear. The distance between individually imagined and actual reality within the attendance of this episode is shattered. Direct communication is the paradigm for the present. This piece is an annunciation devoid of overloaded, magic-infused masks full of vulnerability, wonder, fear, indignation, trust and humility. No plot is further specified. "Whisper" is a universal picture of communication replete with all of the risks. The fragment imparts here the hope that desire does not become objectified through consumerism; that the immaterial (words) be unsatisfactorily replaced with the material, that mutual enjoyment occurs. It is only the gift of love that renders the exchange symmetrical for both parties. CT

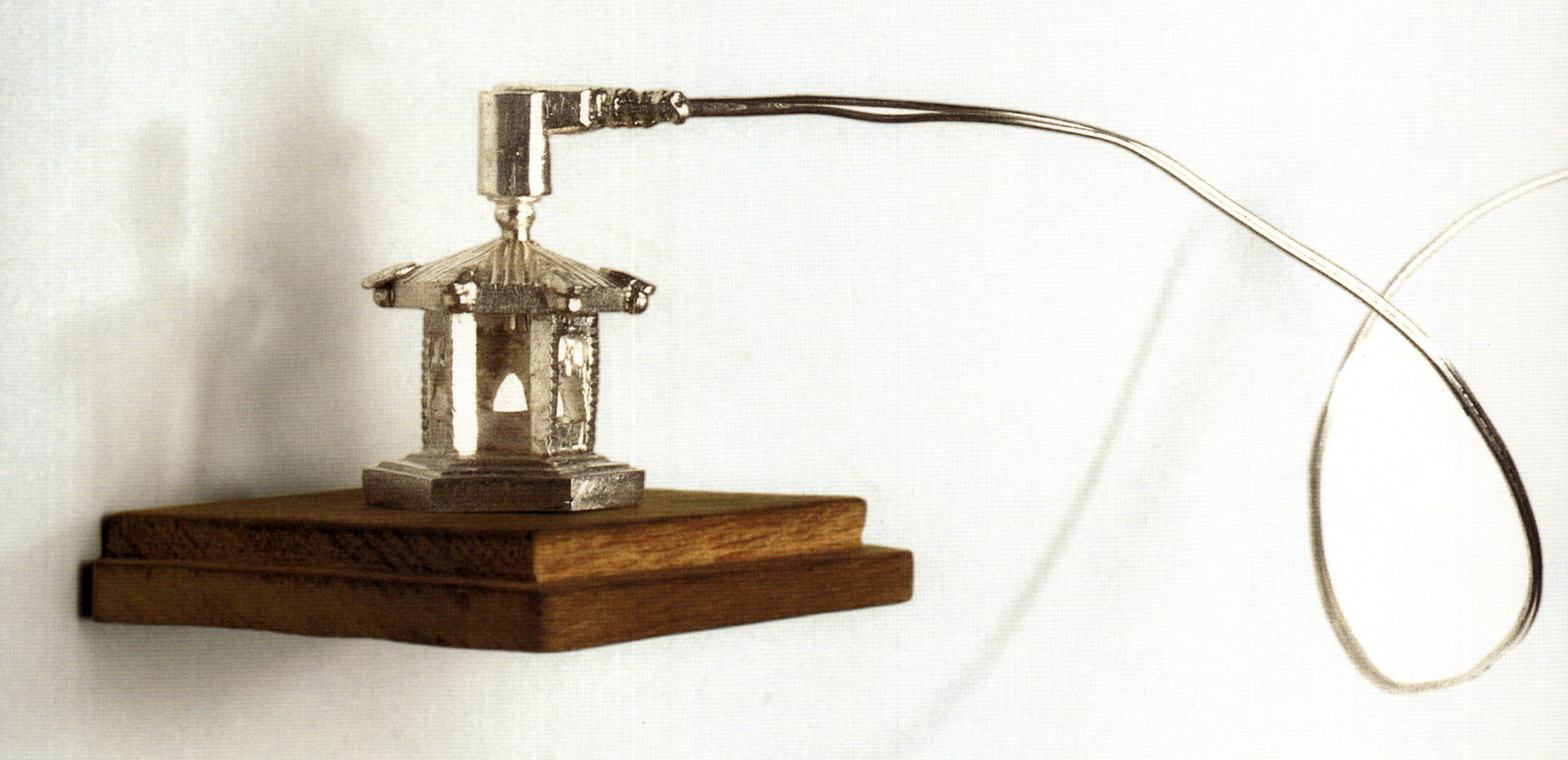

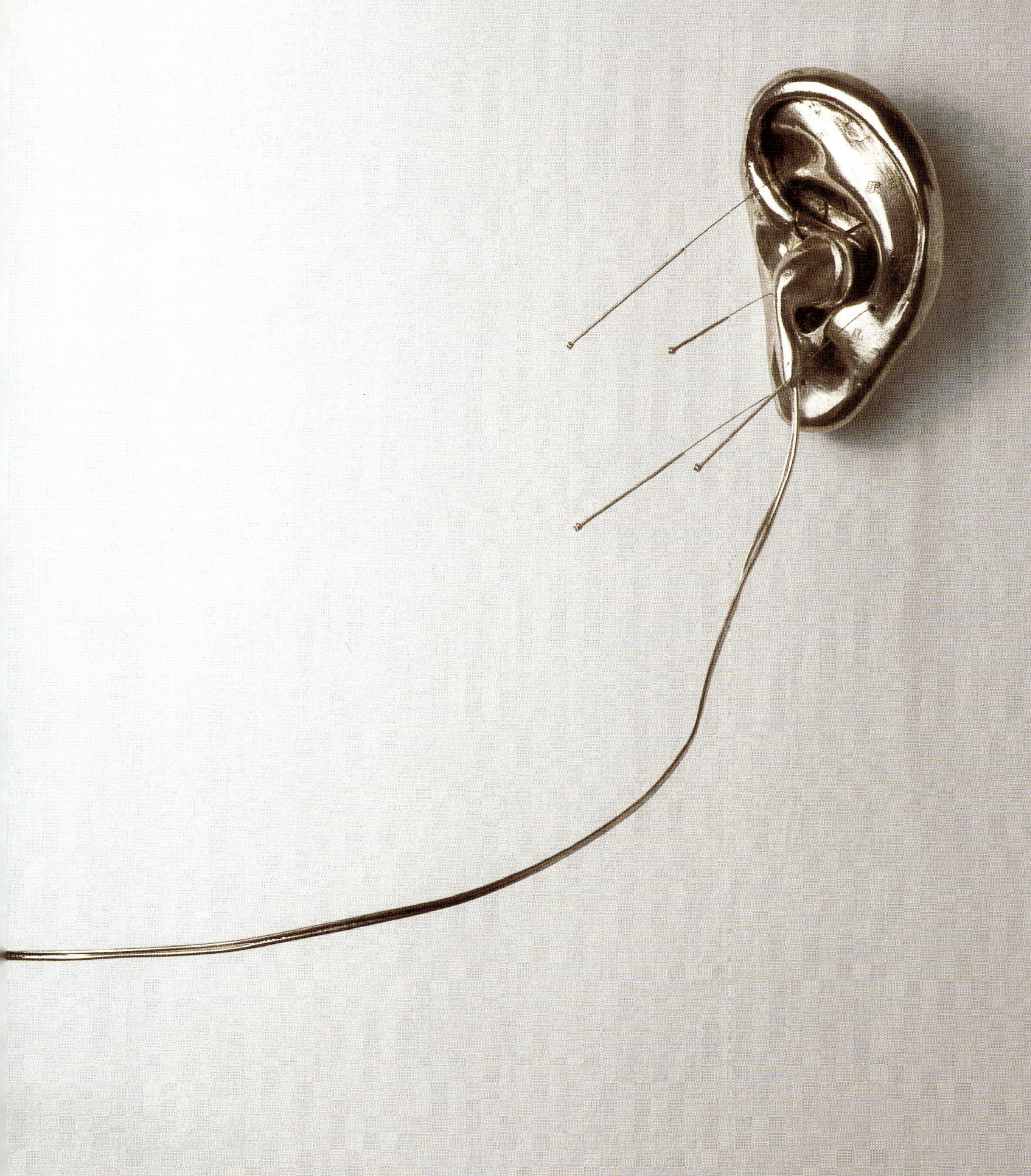

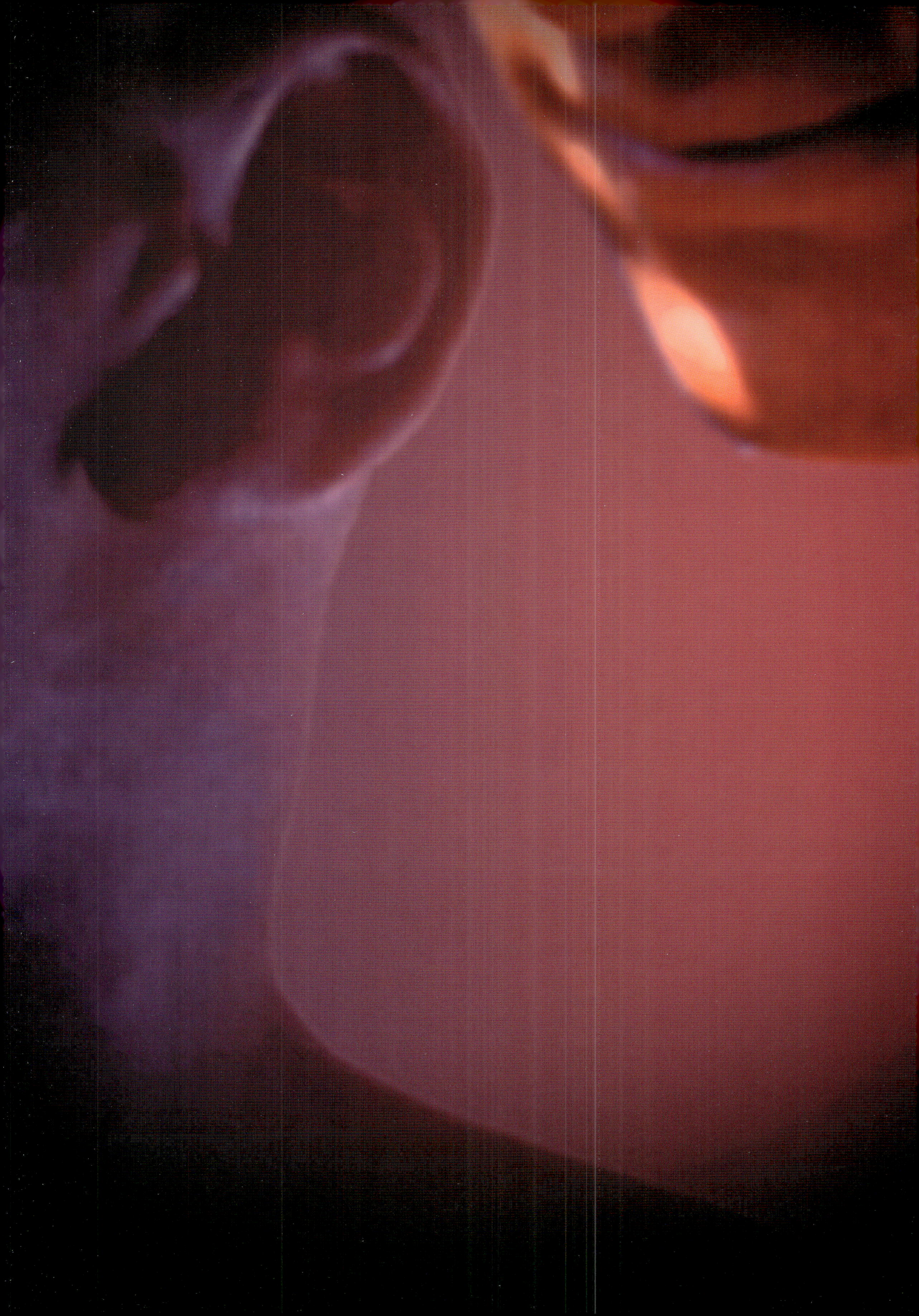

———————— comedy and tragedy ————————

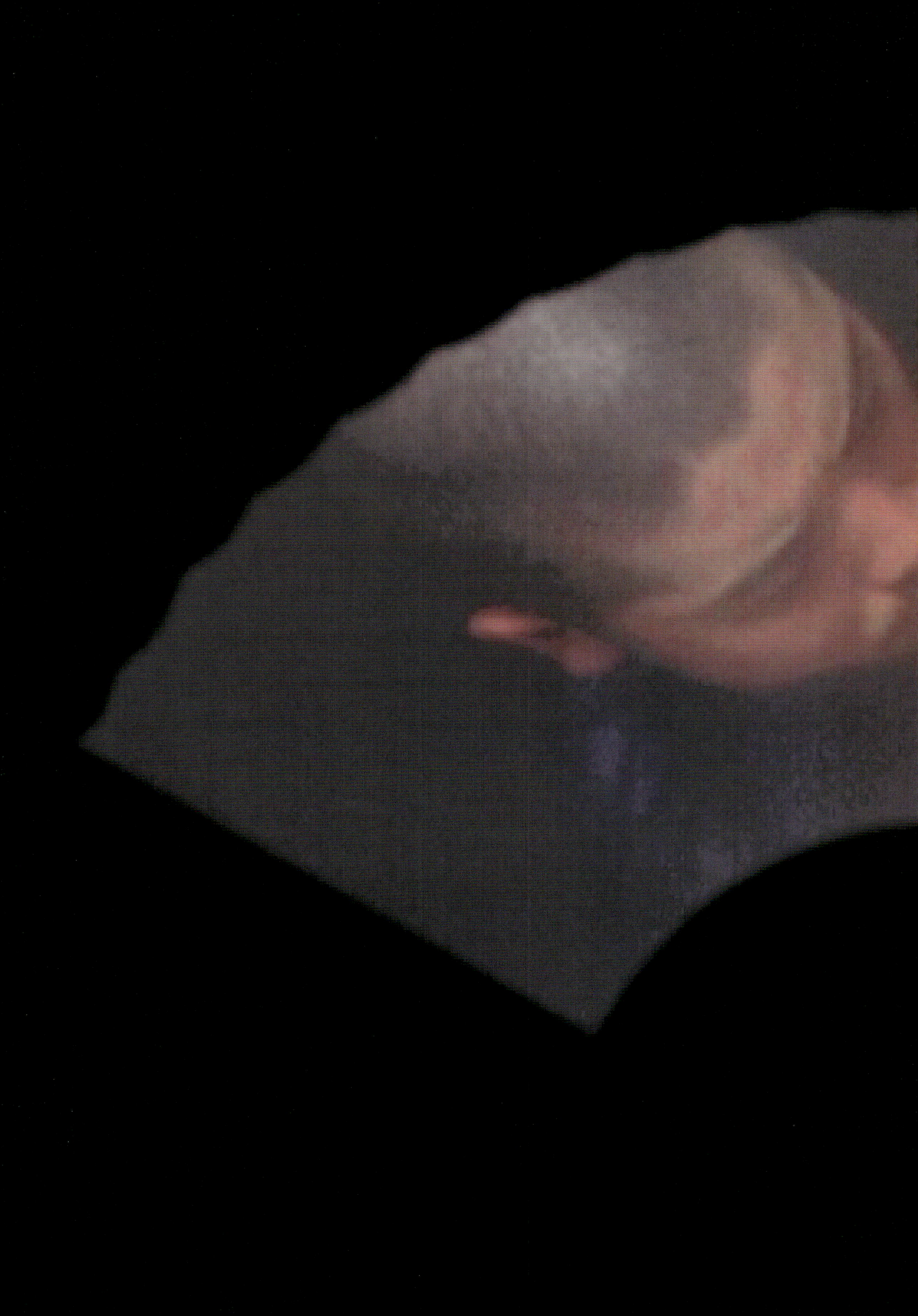

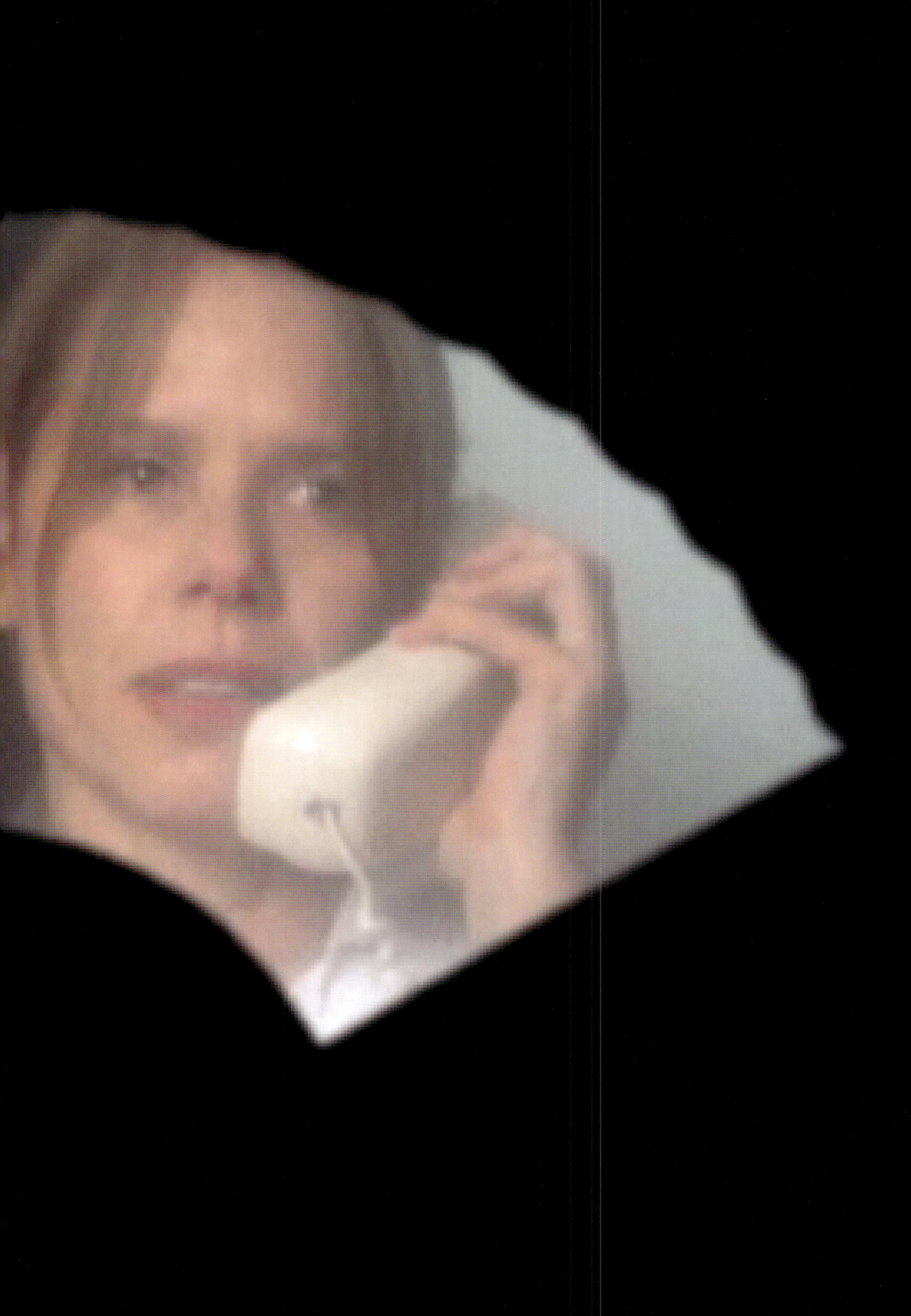

HIMMLISCHE ANWESENHEITEN UND DIE MELANCHOLIE DES VERGÄNGLICHEN IN DEN FILMEN VON MATTHEW WEINSTEIN

Ein Wächterstein

Eine Kaskade

Ein hoher und lieblicher Hügel

Zwei niedrigere Hügel

Ein vierter

Ein fünfter

Ein die Kaskade verschleiernder Baum

Er verdeckt teilweise

unsere Sicht auf das fallende Wasser

Knorrig und verkrümmt

ist er gewachsen und dazu bestimmt

die Auswirkungen von Zeit und Alter anzunehmen

Eine kleine Insel

Sie liegt in der Mitte eines Miniaturteiches

Der Teich wird von unserer Kaskade gespeist

Ein perfekte-Aussicht-Baum

Eine Schneebetrachungslaterne

Die Insel ist mit dem

Hauptland unseres Gartens durch

eine Bretterbrücke verbunden.

Ein Wasserbecken.

Eine Laterne.

Ein Gartenschrein.

Ein Gartentor.

Erlesene Steine.

Sie wurden mit

großem Aufwand und Kosten

aus ganz Japan zusammengetragen.

Sie sind in unserem Garten verstreut.

Sie haben Namen.

Der Kliffstein,

Der Stein der Verehrung,

Der Stein der perfekten Aussicht.

Ich könnte fortfahren,

indem ich die Elemente des Gartens aufzähle und beschreibe.

Aber da ist eine andere Szene, die ich euch zeigen möchte.

Lichter sind in ihren Augen

Und ihre Augen sind wie Lichter ...

CELESTIAL MANIFESTATIONS AND THE MELANCHOLY OF THE TRANSITORY IN MATTHEW WEINSTEIN'S FILMS

A guardian stone.

A cascade.

A high and gentle hill.

Two lower hills.

A fourth.

A fifth.

A cascade screening tree.

It partially obscures

Our view of the falling water.

Gnarled and twisted,

It is grown and bound

to simulate the effects of time and age.

A tiny island,

It sits in the middle of a miniature lake.

The lake is fed by our cascade.

A perfect view tree.

A snow view lantern.

The island is connected

To the mainland of our garden

By a boarded bridge.

A water basin.

A lantern.

A garden shrine.

A garden gate.

Beautiful stones.

They have been brought in

At great effort and expense

From all over Japan.

They dot our garden.

They have names.

The cliff stone,

The worshiping stone,

The perfect view stone.

I could go on and on

Enumerating and exemplifying the elements of our garden.

But there is a different scene that I want you to see.

Lights are in her eyes

And her eyes are like lights …

Eine Kaskade von Wörtern, aneinandergereiht wie Haikus, aus dem Mund eines
Mannes asiatischer Herkunft – wie wir später in „Nemo" erfahren. Ein Sing-sang,
fast Murmeln, monotone Kadenz wie die Yokobue Flöte im Hintergrund. Eine
suggestive Meditation, die in ein Ohr, das man kaum erkennen kann, geflüstert
wird, in einen „Innenraum". Es ist ein Raunen, das verführen soll, der Eingebung
zu folgen, in eine Welt zu entfliehen, die fern ist, unbekannt, ein Garten der Über-
raschungen. Es gilt, einzutreten in einen anderen Ort durch das Tor zum Teegarten,
den Rojimon, – eine Schwelle, die, wird sie übertreten, eine Welt vollkommener
Schönheit, Harmonie und Ruhe offenbart. Die Stimme beschwört die Exterrito-
rialität im Gegensatz zur Gegenwart der geschäftigen Welt, so, als würde das Gedächtnis davon erst die Grundierung für ein Leben in der Gegenwart ermöglichen.
Man folgt den Bewegungen des Mundes des Mannes, eingerahmt von einer über
den Bildschirm gelegten Maske. Sie hat die Form eines Fächers. Der Fächer ist eine
Variation von Möglichkeiten, ein potentieller, gefalteter Raum der Geheimnisse
und der Enthüllung – zusammengefaltet, dunkel und verborgen oder ausgebreitet
und offenbarend. Die Kamera begleitet uns durch den Garten, Abbildungen davon,
sie streift über beschriebene Papiere, das Bildnis einer jungen japanischen Frau,
eine Anhäufung von verschiedenen alltäglichen Dingen: Zigaretten, Zünder…
Das Bild wechselt zu einem anderen Protagonisten, der vom Klingeln des Telefons
aufgerüttelt wird. Zu hören ist die Stimme jenes Mannes, der eben im Traum,
so scheint es, rezitiert hat, wiederholend, dass die Geschichte noch nicht zu Ende
sei und der Protagonist sich zum Fenster begeben solle. Dort angelangt, sieht
er den japanischen Mann auf der Straße, während dieser sich gleichzeitig aus dem
Hinterhalt ihm annähert und mit einem Messer bedroht, vielleicht tötet. Dann
die Vorführung zweier gedachter Varianten der Ermordung durch ein Messer, die
in einer von einem Bild ins nächste verlaufenden lemniskateartigen Taiji-Bewe-
gung experimentiert werden; die zweite Variante beginnt mit dem Messerstoß und
löst sich im Strahl einer spermaartigen Substanz auf, die sich über den Kopf des
Protagonisten ergießt. Dieser bewegt sich von der Ohnmacht (einer Halluzination oder einer Vorahnung) in die Wirklichkeit oder von der Wirklichkeit in einen
retrospektiven Traum (Erinnerung, Gedächtnis). Das lässt sich nicht entscheiden.
Eine Frau spricht ihn an, als er von der unsanften, kleinen Dusche aus dem Traum
gerissen wird. Dieselbe Frau, die in der Imagination des japanischen Mannes
aufgetaucht ist, als Projektion von Schönheit, umgeben von Rosen. Der Protagonist
spricht die Frau darauf an, dass sie wisse wie die Geschichte ausgegangen sei.
Es scheint, als ob eine Transition von ihrem Gedächtnis zu seinem stattgefunden
hätte und er ihre Geschichte aufgrund dieser telepathischen Verbindung kenne.
Er erzählt ihr von Dingen, von denen er nichts wissen kann. Sie ihrerseits erinnert
sich und will den damit verbundenen Schmerz verdrängen und vernichten,
„amputieren", jedenfalls nicht darüber sprechen. Die Erinnerung dränge sich

A cascade of words, strung together, like Haikus, from the mouth of a man of asiatic descent – as we later learn in "Nemo". A sing-song, almost murmuring, monotonic cadence like the Yokobue flute playing in the background. A suggestive meditation, whispered into a barely discernible ear, into an "inner space". It is a humming, a seduction intended to move toward the inspiration, to escape to a world that is remote, unknown, a garden of surprises. It is about entering into another space through the tea-garden gate, the Rojimon – a threshold that, should it be crossed, reveals a world of perfect beauty, harmony and quiet. The voice invokes extraterritoriality, as opposed to the extant frenzied world, as if the remembrance of it would first allow it to become the foundation for a life in the present. One follows the movement of the man's mouth, framed by a mask that is superimposed over the screen. It is in the form of a fan. The fan is a variation of possibilities, a potential, enveloped room of secrets and disclosures – folded over, dark and hidden or spread out and revealing. The camera accompanies us through the garden, depictions of it, it pans over written-on paper, an image of a young Japanese woman, an accumulation of every day objects: cigarettes, matches … The image changes to another protagonist, who is roused by the ringing of a telephone. The voice of the man can be heard – precisely the man, so it seems, from the dream who recites, repeatedly, that the story is not yet finished and that the protagonist should go to the window.

Once there, he sees the Japanese man on the street, simultaneously he is ambushed by the same man, who threatens him with a knife, maybe even kills him. Then follow two imaginary experimental murder variations with the blade, lemniscate-like Taiji movements, which progress from one image into the next. The second variation begins with a knife thrust and dissolves into a stream of a sperm-like substance that sprays over the protagonist's head, who shifts from stupor (a hallucination or premonition) to reality or from reality into a retrospective dream (memory, remembrance). That is not decipherable.

A woman speaks to him as he is roughly pulled from the crude little shower from his dream. The same woman who has appeared in the Japanese man's imagination – a projection of beauty, surrounded by roses. The protagonist then speaks to the woman, that she knows the end of the story.

It appears as if a shift has taken place from her memory to his and that he knows her story as a result of this telepathic connection. He tells her things that he cannot possibly know. For her part, she remembers but wants to suppress and wipe out the pain that goes along with it, "amputate" it, definitely not speak about it. The memory pushes its way to the fore "and fuck[s] you inside-out". The encounter with the stranger could be dangerous: "They're everywhere. We're surrounded by them. Strangers. Just talking to them or even just looking at them is so dangerous. But I do it, I'm doing it all the time."

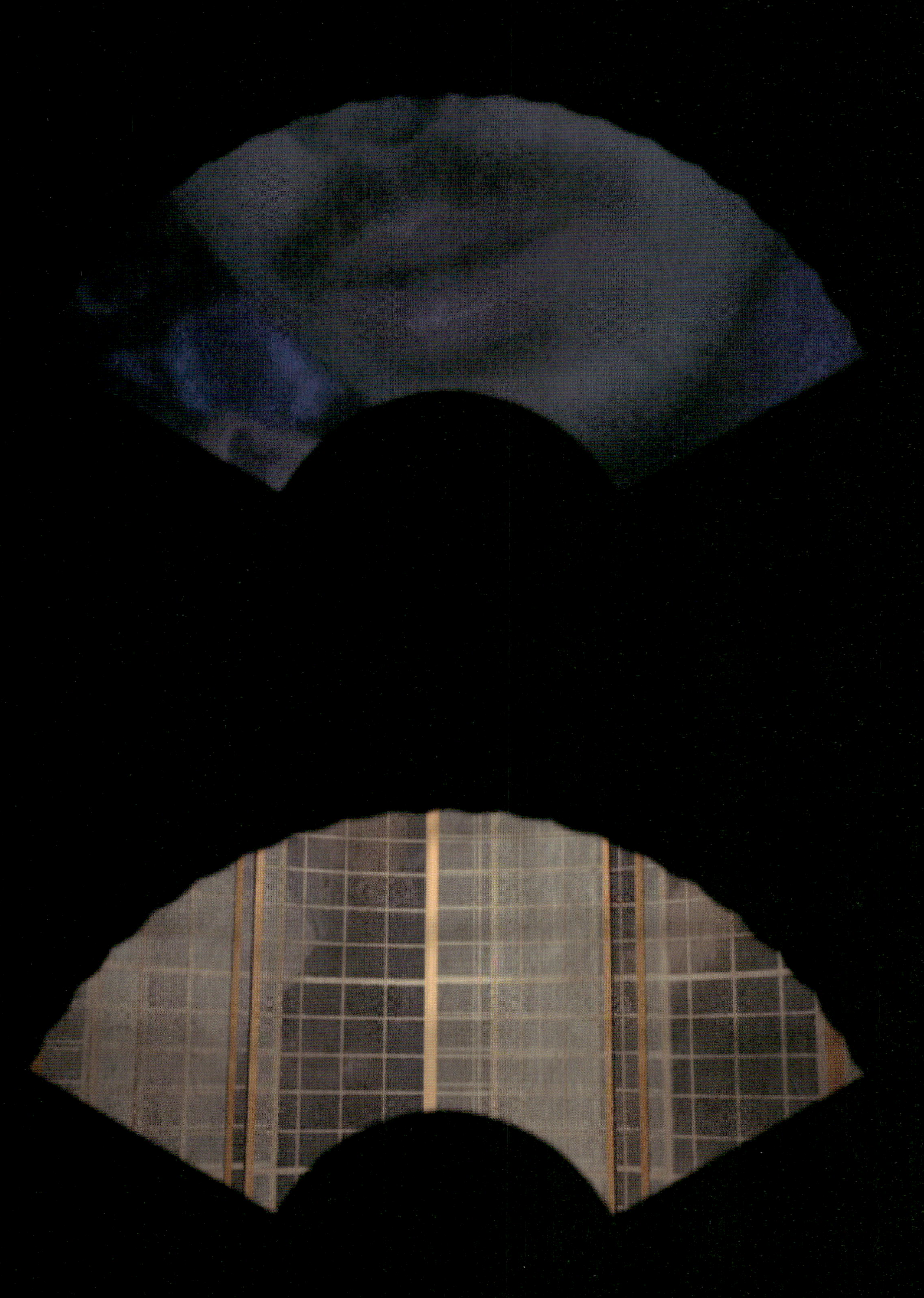

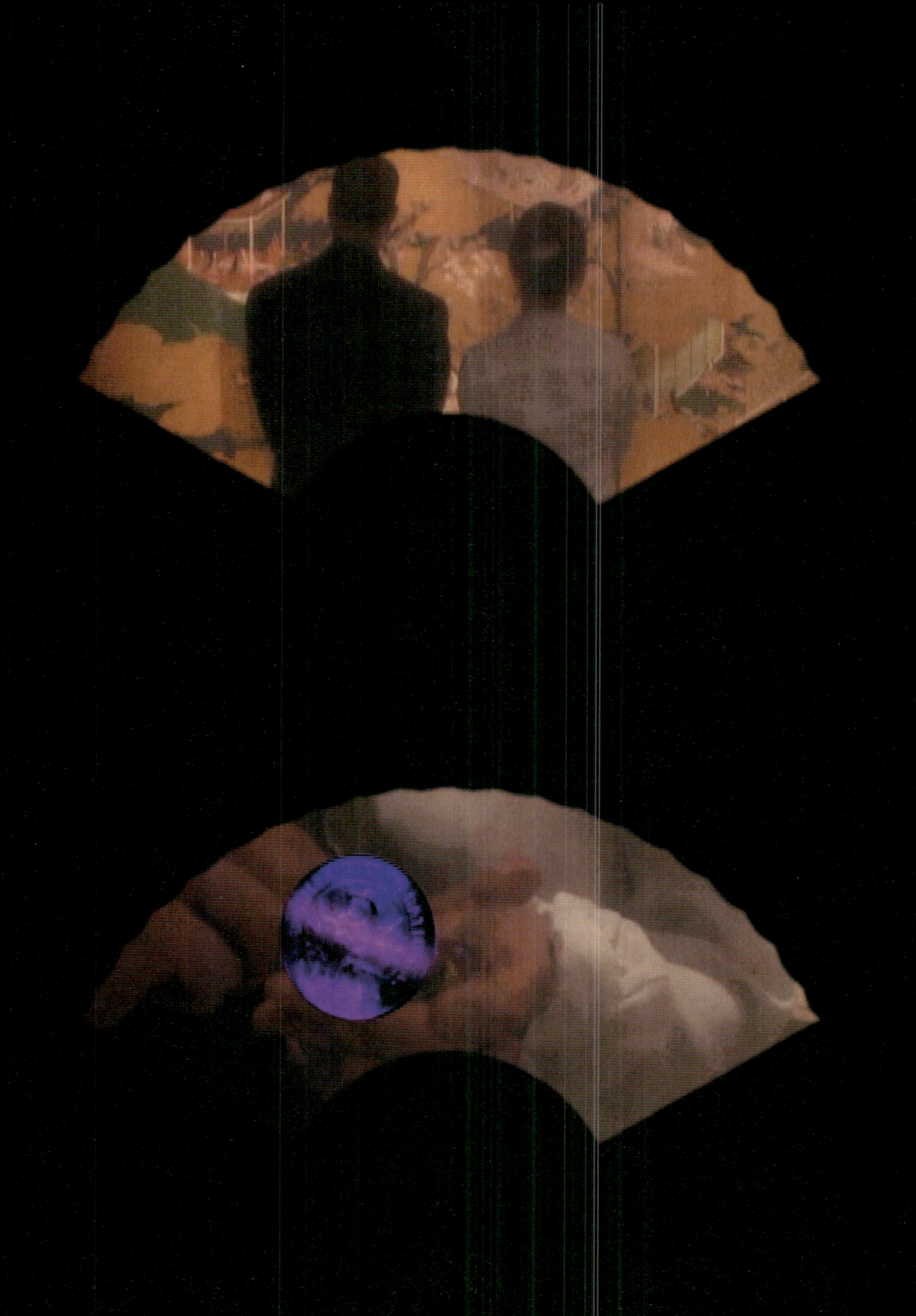

immer wieder ins Bewusstsein und stülpe damit das Innerste nach Außen. Die
Begegnung mit dem Fremden könne gefährlich sein: „Sie sind überall. Wir sind
von ihnen umgeben. Fremde. Allein mit ihnen zu sprechen ist schon gefährlich.
Aber ich tue es, ich tue es die ganze Zeit."

Die Frau erinnert eine Geschichte der Lust und des Todes, die damit beginnt, dass
sie eine farbenfrohe Halluzination vom Himmel fallender Münzen hat – Münzen,
die das Prinzip der Gabe, der Expansion darstellen. Ein psychedelischer Raum der
Verschmelzung von Grenzen. Es ist ein Motiv, das später wieder auftaucht und
mit dem drei weitere Arbeiten von Matthew Weinstein ausgestattet sind: „Rojimon",
das Tor zum Teegarten, eine Schwelle, ein Übergang in eine andere Ebene der
Wirklichkeit (S. 28/29) sowie „Dhalgren" (S. 20/21) und „July 4th" (Vorsatzpapier).
In der nächsten Szene telefoniert die Protagonistin; sie spricht eigentlich mit sich
selbst und reflektiert ihre eigene Einsamkeit, ihre unerfüllten Sehnsüchte, ihren
Mangel an Kommunikation, ihr Bedürfnis nach Berührung. Die Projektion dieses
Bedürfnisses manifestiert sich in einer zärtlichen Kaskade von Küssen, die der
Fremde über ihr Ohr ergießt, während sie mit dem anderen versucht, zu hören,
sich zu verständigen, zu reflektieren, sich zu rechtfertigen. „Glaubst du nicht,
dass ein Rufton eine andere Art von Stille ist? Oder viel mehr als Stille."
In der nächsten Szene treffen sich die beiden Fremden in einem Museum, in der
Abteilung japanischer Kunst. Sie stehen nebeneinander und betrachten einen
antiken japanischen Wandschirm in den prachtvollsten Farben: reich, schillernd,
von meditativer Klarheit.

Er spricht sie an. Sie möchte nicht mit dem Fremden sprechen, kann sich ihm
jedoch nicht entziehen. Er suggeriert ihr, sie wäre daran interessiert, was er in
seinem Aktenkoffer habe und sie imaginiere sicher, er hätte ein Messer darin. Sie
macht den Aktenkoffer auf und entnimmt ihm Gegenstände wie beschriebene
Papiere, eine CD, einen New Yorker Stadtplan, einen Stift, ein Foto von einem
Zen-Garten – dieses macht er ihr zum Geschenk. Er sagt ihr, es gäbe ein Geheimfach („Fach der Einsamkeit") in seinem Koffer mit sprechenden Ingredientien.
Während er sie aufzählt folgt wieder eine Halluzination der farbenprächtigen
Münzen, die er wie um der Szene ein mystische Entrücktheit zu verleihen, in
Zeitlupe in ihre Hand legt als handle es sich um Gaben von unschätzbarem Wert:
eine Rolle Mints, ein Päckchen Kondome, saubere Unterwäsche und Socken,
einen japanischen Roman, Zigaretten, Zünder, das Empire State Building,
ein Bildnis seiner Frau – und ein Messer. Die Münzen fallen in einer helixartigen
Bewegung auf den Boden, parallel dazu folgt wieder die Spirale der Küsse, die
sich über die Frau ergießen. Aus Angst vor Entdeckung an einem öffentlichen,
überwachten Ort flieht sie vor ihrem Begehren und seiner Personifikation.
Der Fächer auf dem Bildschirm wird zu einem Bühnenvorhang von bewegten
japanischen Schiebewänden, shojis, hinter denen die Szene verschwindet und eine

The woman remembers a story of desire and of death, which begins with a multi-colored hallucination of coins falling from heaven – coins that exemplify the principal of reward, of expansion. A psychedelic fusion of boundaries.
It is a motif that will appear again later and finds use in three further works from Matthew Weinstein: "Rojimon", the gate to the Tea Garden, a transition
to another plain of reality (p. 28/29), as well as in "Dhalgren" (p. 20/21) and "July 4th" (endpaper).
In the next scene the female protagonist is on the telephone; she is basically talking to herself pondering her own loneliness, her unfulfilled longings, her lack of communication, her need for physical contact. The projection of these desires manifests itself in a tender cascade of kisses, which the stranger pours fourth around her one ear while with the other ear she tries to listen, to make herself understood, to muse, to justify herself. "Don't you think that a dial tone is another kind of silence? Or much more silent than silence."
In the next scene the two strangers meet in a museum, in the Japanese art section. They are standing side by side and are examining an antique Japanese screen, painted in the most dazzling colors: rich, iridescent, filled with meditative clarity. He talks to her. She doesn't want to talk to strangers, cannot however pull herself away from him. He intimates that she would be interested in what he has in his briefcase and she imagines that he surely has a knife in it. She opens the briefcase and removes papers, a CD, a map of Manhattan, a pen, a photo of a Zen garden – which he then gives her as a present.
He tells her that there's a hidden compartment ("compartment of loneliness") in his briefcase with potent contents. While he enumerates them the colorful coin hallucination returns, which surrounds him and the scene like a mystical reverie, as he, in slow-motion, places the things in her hands as if they were objects of inestimable value: a roll of mints, a package of condoms, clean socks and under-wear, a popular Japanese novel, cigarettes, a book of matches, the Empire State Building, a photo of his wife – and a knife. The coins fall in a helix-like movement to the floor, parallel to that the spiral of kisses follow, which rain down on the woman. Filled with the fear of being exposed in a public, guarded place she takes flight from her craving and his personification.
The fan on the screen turns into a stage curtain made of moving Japanese sliding partitions, shojis, behind which the scene disappears while another appears: the bedroom of the female protagonist. She is awaken by a telephone call from the stranger who bids her to look out the window, while he approaches her from the "trap". What then happens is left to the imagination.
After the encounter of the two she sits, listening, on a chair, blood dripping over her head, throat, the red negligee, her gaze irresolute between vacant and suffering, as if a crown of thorns has been placed upon her head; he is laying on the bed

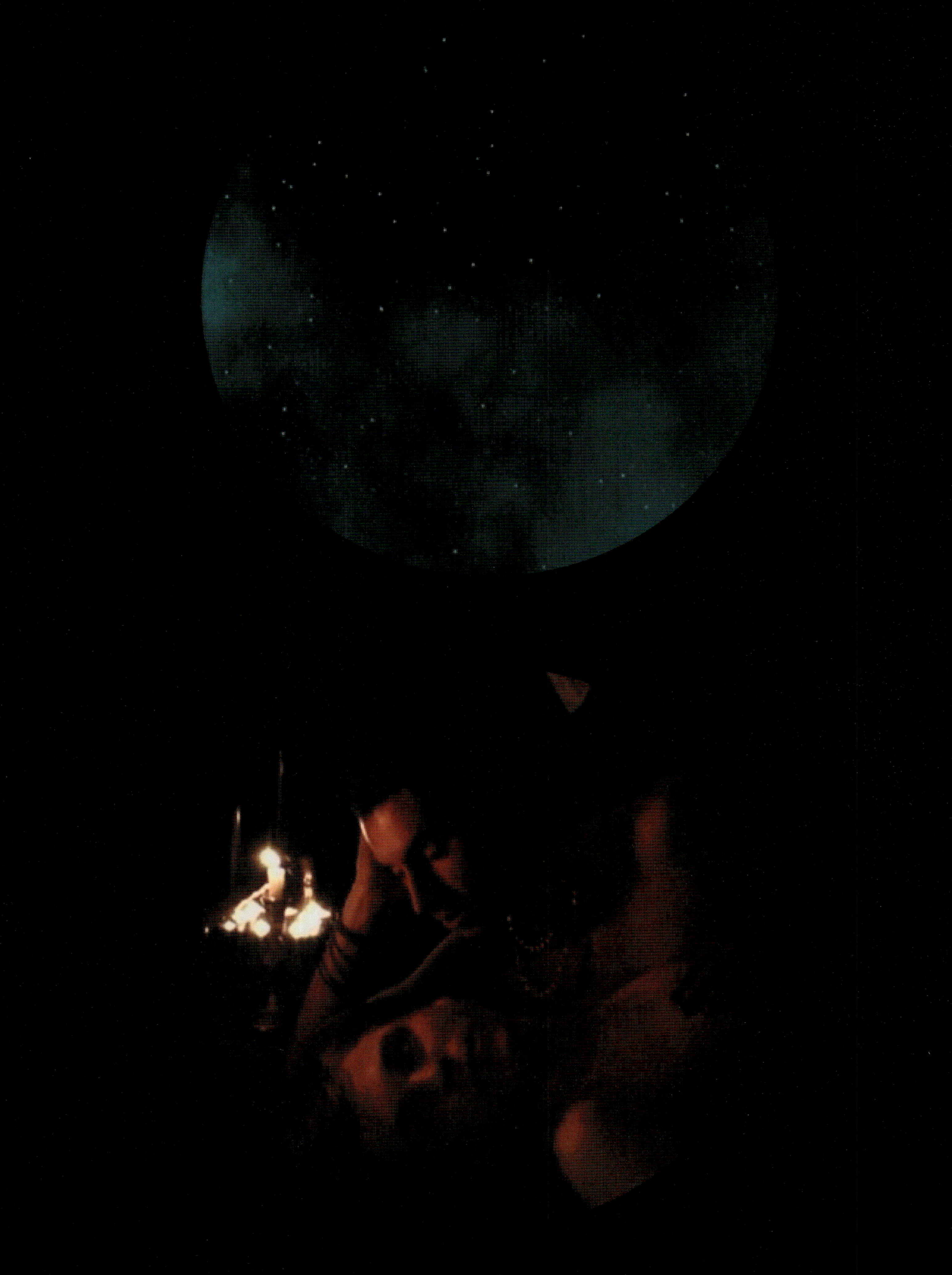

clad in his underwear, awoken from a wake-up service, as he must attend a meeting.
A monologue of self-accusation directed at the woman follows, which is simultaneously an attempt to justify his betrayal. Far from home he feels lonely and
this city is full of people who are also willing to spend a night with a stranger in
order to banish their solitude.

He has to attend the meeting, as a weighty decision will be made there, which is
of great importance for the company. He has to fulfill his duty, after all his family
has expectations and are used to a certain standard of living, etc. His last
sentence, "Are you listening to me?" is aimed at a person who has remained a
stranger to him, with whom he sought a moment of relief from his solitude,
as she also did. He will take his leave and leave her behind — he, full of guilt feelings, she with a feeling of being left behind and an even greater feeling of
loneliness. The angel of desire, transfigured to the angel of death, is parting —
and she cannot hold him back.

The parallel-world theme is also central in Weinstein's film "Ceiling Fan" (2002):
those of Neptunian transcendence and "celestial presences", projections of the
unobtainable versus those of the corporeal, of the covetous, the procreative desire for
eternal beauty and also of inability, transitoriness, finally to accept humanity as such.
The circle as motif appears previously in "Ceiling Fan". A mundane device, the
ceiling fan, is transformed into a halation through its rotations, an emanation of
the divine, of perfection. A perfection, a necessary (dis)illusion, since it is ideal
and superhuman.

While the protagonist has a vision of coming together with a man — the
embodiment of beauty, strength and life — the fan dissolves into a kind of optical
illusion, into a transcendental sea of light.

A moment of transubstantiation: something "celestial" appears and for an instant
is converted into something fleshly in order to deliver a message, as in the Supper at
Emmaus during which Christ appears to his disciples — a spirit ripened into reality.
An absurd and at the same time "innocent" story of divine revelation is spun
around this event. The protagonist is appalled that the hotel in which he had his
vision is to be demolished; that the place where the amalgamation of carnality
and transcendence happened, is to disappear and with it the connection to the
subliminal ethereal world — the collapse of a world that hoisted him into spheres
of all-encompassing love and harmony. The thought is frustrating, as conscious-
ness cannot bear the shortcomings of earthly reality.

Dialogues with a civil servant, a fortune-teller and a priest follow in which the
protagonist undertakes a reality check. All consider him to be more or less crazy.
Even though they, of all people — dealers of the transcendental who assure the
connection between the pragmatic manifest world and the secret interrelations
that inform our fate — do not believe in miracles.

neue auftaucht: das Schlafzimmer der Protagonistin. Sie wird von einem Telefon-
anruf des Fremden geweckt mit der Aufforderung, sie solle aus dem Fenster
schauen, während er sich ihr aus dem „Hinterhalt" annähert. Was sich danach er-
eignet, lässt sich nur imaginieren. – Nach der Begegnung der beiden Körper
sitzt sie zuhörend auf einem Stuhl, das Blut tropft über ihren Kopf, Hals, das rote
Negligé; der Blick unentschieden zwischen leer und leidend, so als hätte man
ihr eine Dornenkrone auf das Haupt gelegt. Er liegt auf dem Bett, mit einer
Unterhose bekeidet, vom Weckdienst geweckt, weil er zu einer Konferenz muss. Es
folgt ein an die Frau gerichteter Monolog der Selbstanklage bei gleichzeitigem
Versuch der Rechtfertigung für seinen Betrug. Er fühle sich fern von der Heimat
einsam und diese Stadt sei voller Menschen, die ebenfalls bereit wären, die Nacht
mit einem Fremden zu verbringen, um ihre Einsamkeit zu vertreiben. Er müsse
jetzt in die Sitzung, weil dort über eine Sache entschieden würde, die für die
Gemeinschaft von großer Wichtigkeit sei. Er müsse seine Pflicht tun, weil seine Familie Erwartungen an ihn hätte, einen bestimmten Lebensstandard gewohnt sei
etc. Sein letzter Satz „Hörst du mir zu?" richtet sich an eine Person, die ihm fremd
geblieben ist, bei der er für einen Moment Entlastung für seine Einsamkeit gesucht
hat wie sie auch. Er wird wieder gehen und sie zurücklassen – er voller Schuld-
gefühle, sie mit dem Gefühl des Verlassenseins und der noch größeren Einsamkeit.
Sie kann den Engel der Lust, der zum Engel des Todes wird, nicht halten.
Auch in Weinsteins Film „Ceiling Fan" (2002) geht es um Parallelwelten: jene
der neptunischen Transzendenz und der himmlischen Erscheinungen („celestial
presences") als Projektion des Unerreichbaren gegen jene der Körper, des Begehrens, der Wunschproduktion von ewiger Schönheit und also des Unvermögens,
Vergänglichkeit, letztlich Menschlichkeit, anzuerkennen. Bereits in „Ceiling Fan"
taucht das Motiv des Kreises auf. Das profane Gerät des Ventilators verwandelt
sich durch sein Kreisen in einen Heiligenschein, einer Emanation des Göttlichen,
der Perfektion. Eine Perfektion, die (ent)täuschen muss, weil sie ideal und
übermenschlich ist. Während der Protagonist die Vision hat, sich mit einem Mann,
Inbegriff von Schönheit, Kraft und Leben, zu vereinigen, löst sich der Ventilator
in einer Art optischen Täuschung in einem transzendenten Lichtermeer auf. Es
handelt sich um ein Moment der Transsubstantiation: etwas „Göttliches" erscheint
und wird für einen Moment fleischlich, um eine Botschaft zu überbringen,
wie im biblischen Mahl zu Emmaus, in dem Christus den Jüngern erscheint. –
Ein Geist, der Wirklichkeit wird.
Um dieses Ereignis herum spinnt sich eine gleichermaßen absurde wie
„unschuldige" Geschichte göttlicher Offenbarung. Der Protagonist ist entsetzt,
dass das Hotel, in dem er seine Vision hatte, abgerissen werden soll, dass also
der Ort des Vereinigung fleischlicher Lust und Erfahrung von Transzendenz verschwindet und damit die Verbindung zur subliminalen Welt des Ätherischen,

Miracles have a price: every question costs five dollars, says the fortune-teller who tells him to go home and live his life, while the priest believes that we all have already used up our miracles and that there are definitely no more to be had. The projection of absolute happiness, of absolute beauty follows disillusionment. Exceptional places, dreams are sacrificed to the entertainment industry, to the production of artificial experiences: "Golden Pagoda" is the name of the structure, which is going to be erected. And the disco-ball with its thousands of beguiling mirrors and lights, invokes the impulse to overlook the self in a music and drug rush, in order to be able to experience the dream of ecstasy, immortality and the dispersal of boundaries.

Both films deal with parallel worlds of desire, with the dream of union and disintegration within another or within the eternal while simultaneously confronting the boundaries of reality, which have been distorted by responsibilities, expectations, guilt feelings and fear. In "Nemo" the personification of the foreign branches off into two directions. It portrays the perilous, which requires protection and in present-day America that which is foreign stands for the ultimate threat. If it were the Japanese in the 1940's who were considered a menace and out of fear interned in quasi "reservations", then today it is the Arabs who are looked at as the embodiment of evil.

The film's second direction shows the fear of the foreign coupled simultaneously with fascination, a certain flirtation with violation. Here the foreign is sexually connoted. As it so often is, the foreign instills fear, but is also exotic, wild, untamable, unapproachable, overwhelming. Fear and desire are hard to separate from each other. The mistrust may be great, but the temptation to open "hidden compartments", to be at risk, and to put trust to the test is all very seductive. The visible, the easily detectable, seems boring, safe – the actual Other is concealed in the hidden compartment. The foreign is always dangerous as it is uncontrollable and operates according to other rules and regulations. The foreign brings with it another cultural background, other archetypical behavior vis-à-vis encounters with the opposite sex. As exciting as that may be, the confrontation with a foreign codex can be destructive, even deadly.

From a social standpoint the act of exclusion is ancient – the stranger is sent out into the wasteland, a scapegoat for non-integration and society is supposedly off the hook; the actual economic and religious reasons remain misapprehended. This duality is maintained in order to uphold the belief of being in the right. Instead of it being seen as two sides of the same coin, it is interpreted as the conflict between good and evil. The Other is used in order to uphold the consistency of the own system.

In any case foreignness is, with reference to the effect on the sexes, the basis of desire arousal – and the foreigner of exotic appearance and different cultural

die ihn in die Sphäre allumfassender Liebe und Harmonie gehoben hat, zusammenbricht. Die Vorstellung ist frustierend, weil das Bewusstsein die Unzulänglichkeit der irdischen Realität nicht erträgt.

Gespräche mit einer Maklerin, Wahrsagerin und einem Priester folgen, in denen der Protagonist einen realitiy check erproben will. Alle halten ihn mehr oder weniger für verrückt. Obwohl gerade sie Händler des Transzendenten sind und die Verbindung zwischen der pragmatischen Welt der Erscheinungen und den geheimen, unser Schicksal bestimmenden Zusammenhängen herzustellen versprechen, glauben sie nicht an Wunder. Wunder kosten Geld: jede Frage kostet fünf Dollar sagt die Wahrsagerin und er solle nach Hause gehen und sein Leben leben während der Priester meint, dass wir unsere Wunder alle verbraucht hätten und es daher mit Sicherheit keine mehr gäbe.

Der Projektion vom vollendeten Glück, vollendeter Schönheit folgt die Desillusionierung. Besondere Orte, Träume werden der Industrie des Vergnügens, der Produktion des artifiziellen Erlebnisses geopfert: „Golden Pagoda" heißt das Gebäude, das errichtet werden soll. Und die Leuchtkugel, die durch ihre Spiegel und tausend Lichter unsere Sinne betören soll, beschwört den Drang, sich im Rausch von Drogen und Musik zu vergessen, um den Traum von Ekstase, Unsterblichkeit und Auflösung der Grenzen erleben zu können.

In beiden Filmen geht es um die Parallelwelten des Begehrens, dem Traum von Verschmelzung und Auflösung im Anderen oder im Unendlichen bei gleichzeitiger Konfrontation mit den Grenzen der Wirklichkeit, die von Pflichten, Erwartungshaltungen, Schuldgefühlen, Angst verstellt ist. In „Nemo" verzweigt sich die Personifikation des Fremden in zwei Richtungen. Es stellt das Gefährliche dar, dasjenige, vor dem es sich zu schützen gilt und im Amerika der heutigen Tage ist das Fremde die Bedrohung par excellence. Waren es in den 40er Jahren die Japaner, die quasi in „Reservaten" gehalten wurden aus Angst vor ihrer Bedrohung, sind es heute die Araber, die als Inkarnation des Bösen gelten. Die zweite Ebene im Film ist die Angst vor dem Fremden bei gleichzeitigem Faszinosum, der Lust an der Übertretung. Das Fremde ist hier sexuell konnotiert. Wie so oft ist der Fremde angsteinjagend, aber auch exotisch, wild, unbezähmbar, unnahbar, überwältigend. Angst und Lust sind schwer voneinander zu trennen. Das Misstrauen ist groß, aber die Versuchung, die „Geheimfächer" zu öffnen und sich in Gefahr zu begeben, Vertrauen zu erproben ist verführerisch. Das Sichtbare, leicht zu Entdeckende scheint langweilig, ungefährlich, das eigentlich Andere verbirgt sich im Geheimfach. Das Fremde ist immer gefährlich, weil es unkontrollierbar ist, nach anderen Gesetzen und Regeln funktioniert. Der Fremde bringt einen anderen kulturellen Hintergrund mit sich, andere archetypische Verhaltensweisen in bezug auf die Begegnung mit dem anderen Geschlecht. So aufregend das sein kann, so zerstörerisch, sogar tödlich

background offers from a Western perspective, with regard to the Middle Easterners and Asians, an even greater forum for imaginative projection vis-à-vis the archaic, the mysterious, the genuine masculine or feminine, as well as power and obsequiousness.

Illusions of extreme and archetypical behavior appear to be inexorably and deeply seated and so being expose the legitimation and rationale for the causes of friction with the Western mind-set; an attitude that seems to have lost all traces of its intensity through an endless emotional discursiveness. When confronted with the subterranean side of the foreign we thus believe that we have rediscovered a lost part of ourselves – perhaps a submerged story of lives – which we formerly lived. However this confrontation implies as well the emergence of the hurtful and even of devastation.

The issues, which Matthew Weinstein addresses in both of his films concern mortality, the projected feeling of one's own finiteness onto something that goes beyond self-existence, transcendental, and the parallel attempt to carry the transcendent experience into the present and, in so doing, bring it into everyday life, with its concretization, busyness and alienation, instilling a bit of authenticity. Fear of the foreign and the concurrent hunt for it are an attempt to shed light on one's own identity, to integrate the borderline experiences of desire, defense, danger and of death as shadows in the self.

SABINE FOLIE

kann der Ausgang in der Begegnung mit dem fremden Codex verlaufen. Gesellschaftlich gesehen ist der Mechanismus der Ausgrenzung uralt, der Fremde wird als Sündenbock für das Nicht-Integrierbare in die Wüste geschickt und damit wird die Gesellschaft von ihren eigenen Widersprüchen vermeintlich entlastet; die eigentlichen Ursachen ökonomischer und religiöser Natur bleiben unverstanden. Die Dualität wird aufrechterhalten, um sich selbst im Recht zu wähnen. Sie wird als Gegensatz von Gut und Böse und nicht als zwei Seiten einer Medaille interpretiert. Der Andere wird benutzt, um das eigene System widerspruchsfrei zu halten.

In Bezug auf das Wirken der Geschlechter ist die Fremdheit der Grund für die Entfachung des Begehrens überhaupt, und der Fremde mit exotischem Aussehen und anderem kulturellen Hintergrund bietet gerade aus dem Blickwinkel westlicher Denkweisen gegenüber orientalisch-asiatischen noch um vieles mehr Projektionsflächen für Imaginationen des Archaischen, Geheimnisvollen, genuin Männlichen oder Weiblichen, Stärke oder Unterwürfigkeit. Vorstellungen von extremen und archetypischen Verhaltensweisen, die unerbittlich und tief verwurzelt erscheinen und damit Legitimation und Grund von Reibungsflächen mit einer westlichen Sichtweise offenbaren, die in der endlosen Diskursivität der Gefühle das eigentliche Spüren ihrer Tiefe verloren zu haben scheint. In der Begegnung mit dem Untergründigen des Fremden glauben wir also einen verlorenen Teil unseres Selbst wieder zu finden, vielleicht eine verschüttete Geschichte der Leben, die wir vor diesem gelebt haben. Aber diese Begegnung impliziert auch das Auftauchen von Schmerzhaftem und Vernichtendem.

Die Fragen, die sich Matthew Weinstein in seinen beiden Filmen stellt, sind die Fragen nach der Sterblichkeit, der Projektion des Gefühls der eigenen Endlichkeit auf etwas, das über die eigene Existenz hinausgeht, etwas Transzendentes und dem gleichzeitigen Versuch, die transzendente Erfahrung in die Gegenwart zu tragen und damit in den prosaischen Alltag in seiner Verdinglichung, Geschäftigkeit und Entfremdung ein Stück Authentizität hereinzuholen. Die Angst vor dem Fremden und die gleichzeitige Suche danach ist der Versuch, unsere Identität zu klären, sie in der Grenzerfahrung des Begehrens, der Abwehr, der Gefahr, des Todes als Schatten in das eigene Selbst zu integrieren.

SABINE FOLIE

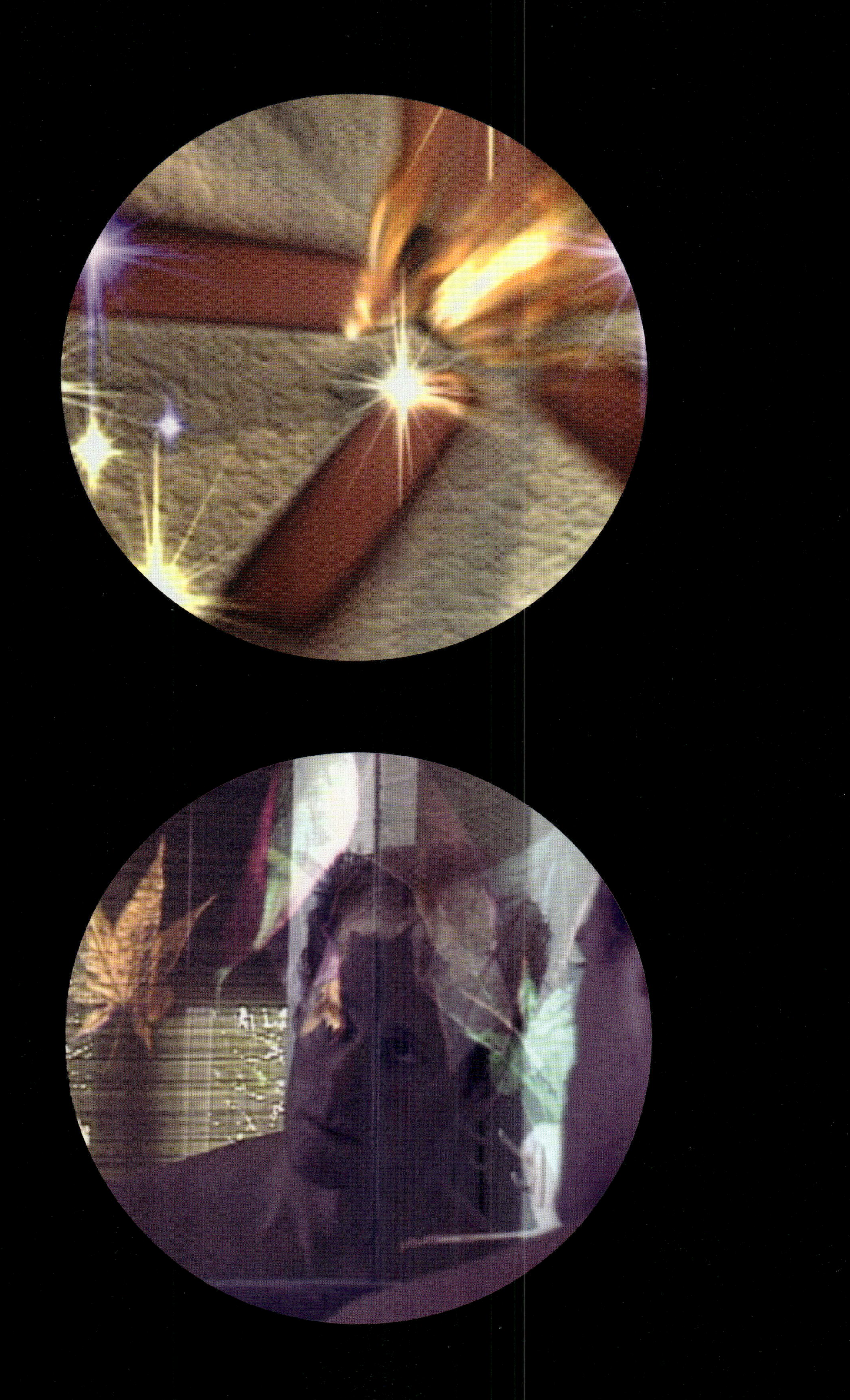

LIST OF WORKS ——————— WERKLISTE

Endpaper / Vorsatzpapier: **July 4th** / **4. Juli**, 2003

Print on fabric, mounted on plexiglass / 47,5 x 58,5 inches

Druck auf Textilgewebe, auf Plexiglas aufgezogen / 120,5 x 148 cm

p. 4/7: **Apples** / **Äpfel**, 2000

Bronze, paint / 93 x 93 x 19 inches / 2001 acquired

Bronze, Farbe / 236 x 236 x 48 cm / 2001 erworben

Pinakothek der Moderne, Sammlung moderne Kunst, Inv. Nr. B 896

p. 8/9: **Black Leaves** / **Schwarzes Laub**, 2003

Print on fabric, mounted on plexiglass / 50 x 61,5 inches

Druck auf Textilgewebe, auf Plexiglas aufgezogen / 127 x 156 cm

p. 12/13: **Snowy Day**, 1996

Acrylic and process inks on canvas and polyester / 94 x 144 inches

Acryl und Siebdrucktinte auf Leinwand und Polyester / 239 x 366 cm

p. 16/17: **Golden Delicious**, 1997

Print on canvas / 36 x 36 inches / Private Collection

Druck auf Leinwand / 91,5 x 91,5 cm / Privatbesitz

p. 20/21: **Dhalgren**, 2003

Dyed silk / 198 x 198 inches

Gefärbte Seide / 503 x 503 cm

p. 22: **Bell** (Bronze Frisbee) / **Glocke** (Bronze-Frisbee), 2003

Bronze / 9,5 x 1 inches / Edition of four, one Artist's Proof

Bronze / 24 x 2,5 cm / Multiple, vier Exemplare, ein Künstlerexemplar

p. 26/27: **Ed Headrick, Designer of the Modern Frisbee, Dies at 78** / **Ed Headrick, Designer des modernen Frisbee, stirbt mit 78**, 2003

Colored Sand / Dimensions variable / Installation in the Pinakothek der Moderne

Farbiger Sand / Maße variabel / Installation in der Pinakothek der Moderne

p. 28/29: **Rojimon**, 2003

Cast iron, set screws, bronze, paint, lacquer / Dimensions variable / Installation in the Pinakothek der Moderne

Gusseisen, Schrauben, Bronze, Farbe, Lack / Maße variabel / Installation in der Pinakothek der Moderne

p. 31: **Shower** / **Dusche**, 2003

Colored Sand / Dimensions variable / Installation in the Pinakothek der Moderne

Farbiger Sand / Maße variabel / Installation in der Pinakothek der Moderne

p. 34, 37: **My name is Asher Lev** / **Mein Name ist Asher Lev**, 2001

Bronze, chromed bronze, paint, violin strings / 63 x 55 x 18 inches /

Collection of Harald und Daniela Schlawin, Zypern

Bronze, verchromte Bronze, Farbe, Violinensaiten / 160 x 140 x 46 cm /
Sammlung Harald und Daniela Schlawin, Zypern

p. 38: **Springtime in Tokyo / Frühling in Tokio**, 2003
Bronze, copper wire, aluminum, paint / Dimensions variable
Bronze, Kupferdraht, Aluminium, Farbe / Maße variabel

p. 41: **American Gothic**, 2003
Bronze, copper wire, aluminum, paint / 6,25 x 4,25 x 15,75 inches /
Edition of four, one Artist's Proof
Bronze, Kupferdraht, Aluminium, Farbe / 16 x 11 x 40 cm / Multiple,
vier Exemplare, ein Künstlerexemplar

p. 42: **Splashes of Vo-Vomit**, 2003
Bronze, copper wire / 13 x 10,5 x 5 inches / Edition of four, one Artist's Proof
Collection of Ashton Hawkins and John L. Moore, III
Bronze, Kupferdraht / 33 x 27 x 12,5 cm / Multiple, vier Exemplare ein
Künstlerexemplar / Sammlung von Ashton Hawkins and John L. Moore, III

p. 46/47: **Branches / Zweige**, 2003
Dyed silk / 192 x 192 inches
Gefärbte Seide / 487 x 487 cm

p. 50/51: **Fall III**, 2003
Dyed silk / 198 x 150 inches
Gefärbte Seide / 502 x 381 cm

p. 54/55: **Excessive Dreaming / Exzessives Träumen**, 2003
Sterling silver, bronze, silver plate, teak, acupuncture needles / Dimensions
variable / Edition of four, one Artist's Proof
Sterlingsilber, versilberte Bronze, Teakholz, Akupunkturnadeln / Maße variabel /
Multiple, vier Exemplare, ein Künstlerexemplar

p. 57: **Whisper II / Flüstern II**, 2003
Print on fabric, mounted on plexiglass / 59,5 x 44,25 inches
Druck auf Textilgewebe, auf Plexiglas aufgezogen / 151 x 112 cm

p. 60/61, 66/67: Filmstills: **Ceiling Fan / Deckenventilator**, 2002
20 minutes / DVD

p. 74/75: Filmstills: **Nemo**, 2003
28 minutes / DVD

Endpaper / Nachsatzpapier: **Continental Drift**, 2003
Print on fabric, mounted on plexiglass / 47,5 x 58,5 inches
Druck auf Textilgewebe, auf Plexiglas aufgezogen / 120,5 x 148 cm

Matthew Weinstein was born in New York City in 1964. He grew up in
New York City, London and Japan and received his BA from Columbia University
in Art History. He began as a critic for Artforum, and then began painting.
His first exhibitions were at the Postmasters Gallery in New York and the Daniel
Weinberg Gallery in Los Angeles. He is represented by the Sonnabend
Gallery in New York. Over the years, Weinstein has branched out into bronze
casting, 3-D animation and narrative film and digital video.
He also teaches 3-D design masters students at New York University's Center
for Advanced Digital Applications.

Matthew Weinstein wurde 1964 in New York geboren. Er wuchs in New York,
London und Japan auf. Sein Studium der Kunstgeschichte an der Columbia
University schloss er mit dem BA ab. Er schrieb als Kritiker für das Artforum
und begann dann selbst mit der Malerei. Seine ersten Ausstellungen fanden
in der Postmasters Gallery in New York und in der Daniel Weinberg Gallery in
Los Angeles statt. Vertreten wird er von der Sonnabend Gallery in New York.
Inzwischen beschäftigt Weinstein sich auch mit Bronzeguss, 3-D-Animation,
Erzählfilm und Digitalvideo. Er unterrichtet Master-Studenten in 3-D-Design am
New York University's Center for Advanced Digital Applications.

We wish to thank / Dank an
Larry Back, David Bers, Carl Freytag, Kurt Hammelbacher, Cecile Hardy,
Stefan Herzog, Andreas Langenscheidt, Dr. Lee, Patrick von Hagen,
Antonio Homem, Jeffrey Sellers, Marion Sommer, Ileana Sonnabend,
Supersample.com NYC

——— impressum ———

This catalogue has been prepared in conjunction with the exhibition
Dieser Katalog erscheint anlässlich der Ausstellung
Matthew Weinstein – Universal Pictures
Pinakothek der Moderne, München, 14.1.2004 – 7.3.2004
Concept / Konzeption: Corinna Thierolf

Catalogue / Katalog
Texts / Texte: Sabine Folie, Corinna Thierolf
Design / Gestaltung: Schmid.Widmaier Design, München
Translations / Übersetzungen: Alan Forman, München
© 2004 Texts / Texte: Pinakothek der Moderne und die Autoren
© 2004 All Reproductions / Alle Abbildungen: Matthew Weinstein, New York;
except / außer p. 7, 26/27, 29, 30/31, 37, 38, 41, 54, 55 Sibylle Forster,
Bayerische Staatsgemäldesammlungen, München;
p. 22 Haydar Koyupinar, Bayerische Staatsgemäldesammlungen, München;
p. 4, 34, 42 Larry Beck, New York
Production / Gesamtherstellung: Kerber Verlag, Bielefeld
Published by / Erschienen im: Kerber Verlag, Bielefeld

Exhibition / Ausstellung
Exhibition office / Ausstellungssekretariat: Birgit Keller
Restoration / Restauratorische Betreuung: Erich Gantzert-Castrillo,
Maike Grün, Lars Raffelt, Florian Schwemer, Susanne Willisch
Installations / Aufbau: Dietmar Stegemann sowie Hilde Heigl,
Wolfgang Kaiser, Anna Leonie und Martin Schmitt
Registrar: Simone Kober
Press and PR / Presse und Public Relations: Tine Nehler, Angela Seemüller
Visitor services / Besucherdienst: Susanne Kudorfer, Anja Zechel
Events / Veranstaltungen: Andrea Pophanken, Barbara Siebert

www.pinakothek-der-moderne.de

Matthew Weinstein – Universal Pictures, hrsg. von Corinna Thierolf
Mit Texten von Sabine Folie und Corinna Thierolf, Kerber Verlag, Bielefeld 2004

Kerber Verlag, Bielefeld 2004
ISBN 3-936646-55-4
Printed in Germany

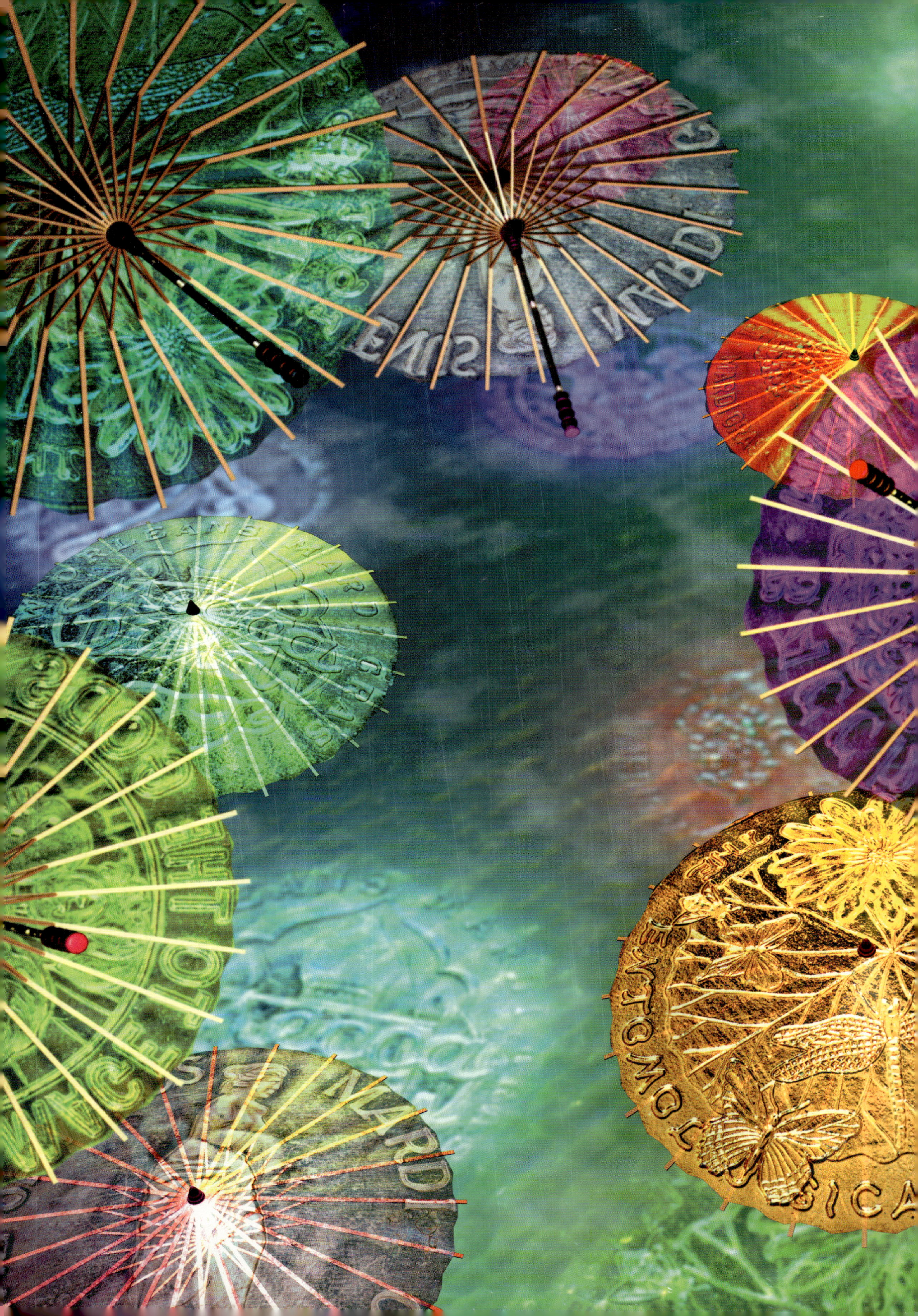